THE 2010 RHYSLING ANTHOLOGY

THE BEST SCIENCE FICTION, FANTASY & HORROR
POETRY OF 2009

THE 2010 RHYSLING ANTHOLOGY

THE BEST SCIENCE FICTION, FANTASY & HORROR POETRY OF 2009

Edited by Jaime Lee Moyer

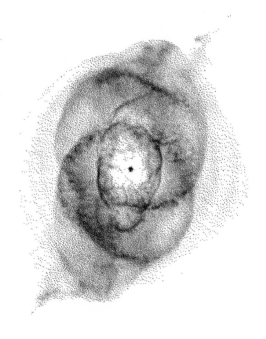

The Science Fiction Poetry Association

The 2010 Rhysling Anthology

Editor and Rhysling Chair: Jaime Lee Moyer

Layout and typesetting: Jon Stout

Cover Photography: "The Cat's Eye Nebula" by NASA, ESA, HEIC, and The Hubble Heritage Team (STScI/AURA)

Cover Design: Mike Allen & Jon Stout

Published by: The Science Fiction Poetry Association, in cooperation with Raven Electrick Ink

Printed by: Lightning Source

For information, write to:
Deborah P. Kolodji, SFPA President
10529 Olive St.
Temple City, CA 91780

**For more information on the
Science Fiction Poetry Association visit:**
www.sfpoetry.com

ISBN: 978-0-9819643-2-4

TABLE OF CONTENTS

LONG POEMS FIRST PUBLISHED IN 2009

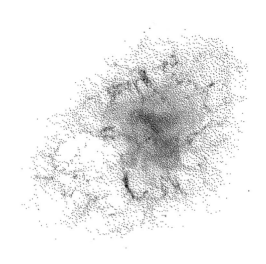

Humans have always had an innate need for stories. We use stories as a way to make sense of the senseless, a way to understand our place in an often baffling world. Those with the knack for storytelling have given all of us the gift of myth and legend, tall tales and epic sagas. They gave us heroes to cheer for, monsters and villains, glimpses of worlds beyond our own. Above all, storytellers gave us a sense of wonder.

My love affair with poetry began with my first reading of Hiawatha at the age of nine. The only poetry I'd known before that was Mother Goose or jump-rope rhymes chanted on the playground. Hiawatha was different.

And it wasn't just the beauty of the language in Longfellow's poem that sparked a lifelong passion in me. What truly amazed me as a little girl was that someone—a poet—could create a world and tell a story with verse, and that this same poet could fill that world with people I came to love. That was magic to me, pure and simple.

What I didn't know at nine was that Longfellow wasn't the first. He was following an ages-old tradition, established by a long line of mythmakers.

For me, that is the essence of what makes speculative poetry and the poets who write it special, and what sets them apart from the larger poetry world. Speculative poets are the keepers of the flame of wonder. They are the new mythmakers.

That is worth honoring.

I was flattered to be asked to edit the 32nd *Rhysling Anthology*, showcasing the poems chosen by members of the Science Fiction Poetry Association as the best published in 2009. Within these pages you will find poems about magic and monsters, physics, visits to the moon, godmothers, airships, and a fragile blue planet rising on the horizon.

Wonders live amongst these pages and myths, newborn.

Enjoy.

—Jaime Lee Moyer
April, 2010

A BRIEF INTRODUCTION ADOPTED
FROM *STAR*LINE* 12.5-6, 1989

In January 1978, Suzette Haden Elgin founded the Science Fiction Poetry Association, along with its two visible cornerposts, the association's newsletter, *Star*Line*, and the Rhysling Awards.

The newsletter cuts straight to Elgin's purpose for founding this organization since it acts as a forum and networking tool for poets with the same persuasion: fantastic poetry, from a science fiction orientation to high fantasy works, from the macabre to straight science, and outward to associated mainstream poetry such as surrealism.

The nominees for each year's Rhysling Awards are selected by the membership of the Science Fiction Poetry Association. Each member is allowed to nominate one work in each of the two categories: "Best Short Poem" (1-49 lines) and "Best Long Poem" (50+ lines). All nominated works must have been first published during the calendar year for which the present awards are being given. The Rhysling Awards are put to a final vote by the membership of the SFPA using reprints of the nominated works presented in this voting tool called *The Rhysling Anthology*. The anthology allows the membership to easily review and consider all nominated works without the necessity of obtaining the diverse number of publications in which the nominated works first appeared. *The Rhysling Anthology* is also made available to anyone with an interest in this unique compilation of verse from some of the finest poets working in the field of speculative/science fiction/fantasy/horror poetry.

The winning works are regularly reprinted in the *Nebula Awards Showcase* published by the Science Fiction and Fantasy Writers of America, Inc., and are considered in the science fiction/fantasy/horror/speculative field to be the equivalent in poetry of the awards given for prose work—achievement awards given to poets by the writing peers of their own field of literature.

Printing and distribution of *The Rhysling Anthology* are paid for from a special fund, the Rhysling Endowment. If you would like to contribute to this fund, please send a check, made out to the Science Fiction Poetry Association and with a notation that it is for the Rhysling Fund, to:

Samantha Henderson, SFPA Treasurer
PO Box 4846
Covina, CA 91723

email: sfpatreasurer@gmail.com

Without the generous donations of many SFPA members, the anthology could not be published.

2010 VOTING PROCEDURES

Use the ballot enclosed with this anthology and mail to the address below by the deadline listed on the ballot:

Jaime Lee Moyer
2889 Neil Avenue
Apt 411C
Columbus, Ohio 43202

You also have the option of voting electronically. Votes for the 2010 Rhysling Award may be sent to **rhysling2010@gmail.com.** Please include your name with your vote as it appears on the SFPA membership rolls.

Make first, second and third place choices for long and short poems. First place votes count 5 points, second place votes are worth 3 points, and third place votes are worth 1 point. You may abstain from making a selection in either category or from any level of choice within a category, if you so choose. You may not list the same poem more than once. The poems with the most points win, and will be reported in a subsequent issue of *Star*Line*.

ACKNOWLEDGEMENTS

Ackerson, Duane, "Outfoxed," *Dreams and Nightmares* #82, January 2009.

Ackerson, Duane, "The Bermuda Triangle," *Star*Line*, July/August 2009.

Agner, Mary Alexandra, "The Glass Ship," *Illumen*, Autumn 2009.

Agner, Mary Alexandra, "Wishes for Godmothers," *Illumen*, Autumn 2009.

Allen, Mike, "Ascending," *Strange Horizons*, January 2009.

Allen, Mike, Evans, Kendall, and Kopaska-Merkel, "Rattlebox III," *Strange Horizons*, July 2009.

Amen, John, Rampage, "At The Threshold Of Alchemy," *Presa Press*, 2009.

Ayers, Lana Hechtman, "The First Story," *Hot Metal Press*, Spring 2009.

Barrette, Elizabeth, "How the Aztecs Conquered Cortés," *Vampyr Verse*, Popcorn Press 2009.

Barrette, Elizabeth, "Fallen Gardens", *Apex Magazine*, April 2009.

Barrette, Elizabeth, "The Dreamgod," *Star*Line*, November/December 2009.

Barrette, Elizabeth, "The Mummy Child," *Star*Line*, September/October 2009.

Beatty, Greg, "eventual, i," *Cinema Spec: Tales of Hollywood and Fantasy*, Raven Electrick Ink, 2009.

Beaudoin, Penny-Anne, "The Magician's Assistant," *Doorways Magazine* #8, April 2009.

Bennefeld, Elizabeth, "Endings", *Star*Line*, July/August 2009.

Bergmann, F.J., "Exobiology II," *Asimov's Science Fiction*, July 2009.

Berman, Paula, "Clotho Visits the Local Yarn Store," *Twist Collective*, November 2009.

Betts, Matt, "Godzilla's Better Half," *Star*Line*, November/December 2009.

Bolden, Emma, "The Witch's Burning," *Guernica*, July 2009.

Borski, Robert, "Scent & Sensibility," *Doorways Magazine* #8, April 2009.

Borski, Robert, "Sweet Tooth," *Strange Horizons*, June 2009.

Boston, Bruce and Simon, Marge, "The Time Traveler Takes His N[th] Lover at a Point of Departure," *Strange Horizons*, January 2009.

Boston, Bruce, "Thirteen Ways of Looking at a Vulture," *Farrago's Wainscot*, October 2009.

Breiding, G. Sutton, "Postcards from Mars," *Star*Line*, July/August 2009.

Brown, Rachel Manija, "Nine Views of the Oracle," *Apyss & Apex*, #32, 4th Quarter 2009.

Bryant, Shelly, "Manipulation," *Scifaikuest*, Online Edition, May 2009.

Casey, Rosalind, "Custody," *Goblin Fruit*, Spring 2009.

Clark, G. O., "Millennial Mass," *Mythic Delirium #20*, Winter/Spring 2009.

Clink, David, "The Airships Take Us, Even As We Blow Out The Last Candle," *Chizine*, Issue #40.

Cooney, C. S. E. and Kornher-Stace, Nicole, "Other Difficulties," *Demon Lovers and Other Difficulties*, published by *Goblin Fruit*, July 2009

Deeley, Malcolm, "Outward, Through the Inner Worlds," *Star*Line*, January/February 2009.

Dietrich, Bryan D., "Edgar Allan Poe," *Asimov's Science Fiction*, November 2009.

Dietrich, Bryan D., "Prince," *The Mayo Review*, Print Edition 2009.

El-Mohtar, Amal and Wick, Jessica Page, "Apple Jack Tangles the Maidy Lac with a Red, Red Ribbon," *Mythic Delirium #20*, Winter/Spring 2009.

Evans, Kendall and Kopaska-Merkel, David, "Corrected Maps of Your City," *Night Ship to Never*, Diminuendo Press, an imprint of Cyberwizard Productions, January 2009.

Evan, Kendall and Henderson, Samantha, "In the Astronaut Asylum," *Mythic Delirium #20*, Winter/Spring 2009.

Evans, Kendall and Wilson, Stephen M., "The Little Sea Maid," *The Book of Tentacles*, Sam's Dot Publishing, December 2009.

Favazza, Angel, "Joyride," *Star*Line*, March/April, 2009.

Files, Gemma, "The Drowned Town," *Goblin Fruit*, Summer 2009.

Forrest, Francesca, "The Qin Golem," *Not One of Us #41*, April 2009.

Frazier, Robert and Joron, Andrew, "Cities in Fog," *Strange Horizons*, November 2009.

Gage, Joshua, "Snow, Blood, Night," *New Myths*, June 2009.

Gailey, Jeannie Hall, "Rapunzel Considers the Desert," *Cabinet des Fées*, Issue 8, September 2009.

Gaiman, Neil, "Conjunctions," *Mythic Delirium #20*, Winter/Spring 2009.

Gardner, Delbert R., "The Meek Shall Inherit...(The Earthworm Speaks)," *Goblin Fruit*, Summer 2009.

Gardner, Lyn C. A., "God's Cat," *Sybil's Garage #6*, May 2009.

Gardner, Robert K., "Creation Myth," *Illumen*, Autumn 2009.

German, Wade, "From Tindalos," *Space and Time #109*, Winter 2009.

Hammer, Larry, "At Death's Door," *Ideomancer*, June 2009.

Hinderliter, Carolyn M., "parental pride," *Scifaikuest*, August 2009 Online Edition.

Kopaska-Merkel, David C., "hillbilly invasion," *Sloth Jockey*, January 7, 2009.

Kornher-Stace, Nicole, "The Changeling Always Wins," *Goblin Fruit*, Spring 2009.

Kriesel, Michael, "Fungi from Yuggoth," *Barbaric Yawp*, Vol. 13 #4, October 2009.

Landis, Geoffrey A., "Earthrise, Viewed from Meridiani, Sol 687," *Best Poem*, January 2009.

Lemberg, Rose, "Godfather Death," *Goblin Fruit*," Fall, 2009.

Lindow, Sandra J., "Finding the God Particle," *Strange Horizons*, December 2009.

Lipkin, Shira, "When Her Eyes Open," *Lone Star Stories*, February 2009.

MacFarlane, Alex Dally, "Beautifully Mutilated, Instantly Antiquated," *Goblin Fruit*, Summer 2009.

MacPhearson, Kurt and Yennik, Rick, "Joanie the Jammer," *Tales of the Talisman*, Autumn 2009, Vol. 5, Iss. 2.

Mannone, John C., "Layers of Man," *Liquid Imagination*, Issue 4, Fall 2009.

Mock, Sharon, "Alexander von Humboldt Visits the Moon," *Lunar Maria Poetry Contest*, September 2009.

Moore, George, "Triangulation," *Astropoetica: Mapping the stars through poetry*," Vol. 7.1, Spring 2009.

Moyer, Jaime Lee, "Nightfall," *Star*Line*, January/February 2009.

Muslim, Kristine Ong, "Conrad, in the Autopsy Room," *Dreams and Nightmares #83*, May 2009.

Muslim, Kristine Ong, "The Tree of Forgiveness," *Paper Crow*, March 2009.

Narayan, Shweta, "Apsara," *Goblin Fruit*, Summer 2009.

Narayan, Shweta, "The Bears Are Working," *Goblin Fruit*, Winter 2009.

Nicola, James B., "Particles and Planets," *The Lyric*, Fall 2009.

Olenich, Olga Pavlinova, "Medea of Melbourne," *Cordite Poetry Review 3.10: Epic*, December 2009.

Rich, Mark, "It Snowed," *The Magazine of Speculative Poetry*," Vol. 8, Iss. 4, Spring 2009.

Rockwell, Marsheila, "Nonrenewable Resources," *Star*Line*, July/August 2009.

Rockwell, Marsheila, "Of Amaranth and Honey," *Paper Crow*, September 2009.

Runolfson, J. C., "Lifestory," *Ideomancer*, March 2009.

Runolfson, J. C., "O.D.," *Goblin Fruit*," Winter 2009.

Saplak, Charles, "Laments of the Lucid Dreamer," *Paper Crow*, September 2009.

Schwader, Ann K., "To Theia," *Strange Horizons*, September 2009.

Simms, Meliors, "Two Kinds of Time," *Voyagers, Science Fiction Poetry from New Zealand* edited by Mark Pirie and Tim Jones, Interactive Press 2009.

Simon, Marge, "For a Few Coins, I Draw you a Picture," *Star*Line*, November/December 2009.

Spelman, Lucien E. G., "Family Jaunt," *Niteblade*, June 2009.

Stanley, J. E., "Cabaret," *Asimov's Science Fiction*, March, 2009.

Stanley, J. E., "City of Bridges," *Sybil's Garage #6*, May 2009.

Stewart, W. Gregory, "My Grandfather's Watch Fob," *Dreams and Nightmares #83*, May 2009.

Summers, David Lee, "A Tale of Three Worlds," *Private International Review of Photographs and Texts*, Summer 2009.

Sykora, Anna, "On Its Own," *Niteblade*, March 2009.

Taaffe, Sonya, "The Chymical Marriage," *Strange Horizons*, August 2009.

Tentchoff, Marcie Lynn, "Owner's Manual," *Tales of the Talisman*, Spring 2009.

Tentchoff, Marcie Lynn, "The Bookseller's Tale," *Illumen, Spring* 2009.

Wilgus, Neal, "Daylight Savings," *Dreams and Nightmares #84*, September 2009.

Wilson, Stephen M., "The Men All Pause (a poem on Global Warming)," *Poet's Espresso*, May 2009.

Youmans, Marly, "Self-Portrait as Dryad, No. 7," *qarrtsiluni*, December 2009.

Outfoxed
Duane Ackerson

A fox in the woods at night
laps at the moon as it passes in the stream.

Suddenly,
the fox is filled with quicksilver light
and finds itself
dashing through the sky,
caught up in a new task:
thread shooting from the eye of a needle,
meteor in reverse
falling up the sky.

Some seam in space
is pulled back together by its passage.
Now it rests in a cage filled with light
neat as a button
caught on a sleeve.

Downstream,
the moon re-collects itself,
continues its journey,
a red gleam in its eye.

The Bermuda Triangle
Duane Ackerson

Perhaps our mistake is thinking of it
as occupying a specific clearcut location.
Try to see it in a fuzzier focus,
as uncertainty made visible.

Having sucked nourishment from WWII aircraft
down to the bones,
it leaves the warm waters of the Gulf
and, like the ancient fish,

begins to move on land.
Then takes to air.

Those watching the skies,
looking closely, can see
of a sort of giant jellyfish,
all but invisible,
far larger than a Portuguese man of war
or any other sea creature.

Caught in the jet stream,
it drifts off over land,
occasionally descending to impersonate
some unexpected, unseasonal tornado.
Small towns begin to disappear.

It gives as well as takes away:
passing over Roswell, New Mexico
it deposits new relics in the UFO Museum.

Elsewhere, taking a turn down a superhiway,
it lifts a car driven by an old lady
and deposits it, pointed the wrong way,
on the other side of the freeway.
Later, she tries to explain
to the patrolman,
is dismissed as another old nut.
No one wonders at her miraculous survival
on the wrong side of things.

Those who like to pin truth to the wall
label it fixed and certain
don't realize it's hard to catch
a moving target
and easy to be caught by it.

The more clear-sighted don't always see this.
Nevertheless, it moves.

Wishes for Godmothers
Mary Alexandra Agner

Tiptoe through the pumpkin patch.
Slippers forgotten, crown cast off
as the couple wends their way,
oblivious to whether you skulk or shout.
The sound of clothes shifting
is the same rough paper song
of winter squash unfurling leaves
in the autumn sun. Don't watch;
there's nothing new to a fairy godmother.
One wand wave and all the problems go,
the girls go, gushing about a prince:
the same one each wish:
handsome, charming. And tall.

You walk home in your sensible shoes,
hang your wings near the umbrella,
open the fridge in the dark kitchen
rooting 'round for the day-old soup.
Midnight gets easier and easier,
but the after hours, awake, dawn
suspended by the ticking of the clock
speeding up and slowing down in rhythm
with the fear inside your heart, become unbearable.
You ache for the dormice coachmen,
the surreal in vivid colors, the poison apple,
your own prince so many stories gone,
dying in his sleep as men worn out
in youth are wont to do. Prettied-up crone,
you no longer cringe at memory,
sweet and bitter. You swing your legs
down off the bed and stand.
There are no wishes left for godmothers.

Ascending
Mike Allen

for Tom Disch

The escalator, rolling ever down,
has reached an end at last and here you lie
as lonely as a sailor left to drown—
like your trapped hero, we cannot know why.

The roaches march in lockstep to commands
like convicts programmed for unwelcome war,
a war that's lost though no one understands
but you, who tried to warn us once before

what lies in wait for red-faced arrogance.
"We are all cripples"—you, alone, divine,
a smirking Momus whose knife-twirling prance
drew blood to fill our cups of dream-dark wine.

Your Resurrection surely won't take long:
your demon words borne high on wings of song.

Fallen Gardens
Elizabeth Barrette

I remember the cradle of civilization
when it was green and growing.
I remember the fertile crescent
when cattle ran like rivers and
grain pattered from the stalks like rain.
I remember sand-lost Sumer and
my priestess heart weeps for Babylon's fallen gardens.
When the barbarians battered down the gates, I was there,
in the temple, pressing "I told you so" into the cold wet clay.

Now history has scrolled along, and
the barbarians are ransacking the temples again.
Salt sparkles in the fields, turning them to dust—
the floods have come and gone,
and nothing grows there now.
Can you harness a river like an ox?

Can you raise green stems from the dust?
Your ancestors, too, thought they knew
but you laugh and sell their bones for beer.

Once again civilization digs its own grave.
Once again the wind scatters my warnings like chaff.
Someday my descendants
may find these words in a trash heap.
I say to them as well,
"Beware: the desert opens itself like a fist.
Already its ancient fingers reach for your land
and you do not even feel its dry papery touch on your heart.
Only I remain, watering the dust with the brine of my tears."

The Dreamgod
Elizabeth Barrette

The Dreamgod walked this world with the other gods in the first days.
Feathers of emerald and aubergine sheathed his body. Peacock plumes
blinked their eyes at nubile maids, their fluttering strands touching the
skin lightly as eyelashes. Two bird-of-paradise quills quivered behind
him, holding between them a gateway to an elusive land. Wheat there
was, too, golden streaks in the green grass of his hair. Flowers there were,
creamy calla lilies whose furled shapes hinted at the intimate parts
of women. Whoever breathed the intoxicating scent of his blossoms
swooned in his arms, dreamswept, as limp as fallen petals. His antlers rose
in a great brown rack, swept back over his broad shoulders, yet delicate
in their geometric perfection. Only his eyes were indistinct, indescribable,
filled with the white silence of starfire.

In the beginning that was how he walked among the gods and the
animals, the First Woman and First Man. Yet he was soon cast from the
world of flesh and stone, the first to lose the fine strange body into which
he had awakened. When the feathers fell from his shoulders, the gateway
to paradise closed. The plants and the animals that picked up the pieces
of his body held, each of them, only a small piece of his magic—Stag and
Peacock, Wheat and Lily. From his bones there grew the first entheogens,
the god-leafed ones—Datura and Amanita, Mescal and crazy old man
Marijuana. They rebuilt the bridge that had been broken, connecting the
world of flesh to the world of spirit. The other gods shrugged and went
on creating order.

But then the other gods, too, began to fade. They became only echoes
in the spirit world, who once had been solid as stone. The Dreamgod
said nothing. He merely spread his ghost feathers against the evening sky
and painted it with colors. He breathed through a stand of reeds, then
watched First Boy cut the music free from them as he made the first flute.
When First Girl came to her womanhood, he kissed her with the flavor
of fermented honey on his lips, and watched her wander away to invent
mead. Long after the other gods had been forgotten, their tasks complete,
the Dreamgod remained.

He still lives today, a half-step away from the world of flesh and stone. For
creation and chaos are never finished.

The Mummy Child
Elizabeth Barrette

It is the hand that haunts me.

It is the dark, dry, withered hand
that clenches around my finger.

It is the fragile, parchment-skinned hand
that paws at my palm.

It is the desperate, hungry, dying hand
that scrabbles after food I do not have.
> *We were not allowed to share our own food.*
> *Even if it went to waste.*
> *Rules, you know.*

It is the hand that haunts me,
the hand of the child I could not save,
and not, oddly, the whole child,
though that memory too is perfectly clear.
> *The little mummy child lay in the hole,*
> *as dessicated as the sand itself,*
> *sharp bones poking at the black skin.*
> *There was no cloth for wrappings.*

Each month, the same dream returns:
I remember those long weeks in Africa
that shriveled the hope in my heart

like a seed left in the pitiless desert sun.
I remember the hand, so tiny and frail,
yet so terribly strong.
I hear again the strange creaking cry,
like the sound of old leather bending.
The flesh has drawn back from the small hard nails,
which claw across my belly and leave me bleeding.

It is the hand that haunts me,
scooping the life out of me,
wringing me out too dry even for tears.
 So no,
 I don't think I'm expecting.
 I have no expectations at all.

eventual, i
Greg Beatty

Videos, the sign declared
in daylight, in gleaming
plastic. All very clear,
and all very commercial.
But after Tuesday, at night
it read ideos. Is this become
a store of ideas? Of uniqueness?
Of uniqueness…for rent?
In daytime, people still rent videos.
At night, though, bright colors,
flaring memes, and revolution's sold.
A week, then it became an
ide s store, a looming mid-month
threat from verse and history;
dour robed figures arrive at twilight.
Are those daggers clutched
in blank-stained hands? What's the
fated overdue charge on an ide?
A week of suns, and night
winds make the store an
id shop. The fiercely unclothed
crowd went wild, tearing
dark ribbons and one
another from careful cases

to sprawl upon the sidewalk.
In daylight I rent *Earnest*
Goes to Camp and *Citizen*
Kane and wait, until at last
the store becomes what I know
it will, an eventual i shop
where at last i'll rent
identity, bereft of others
and other letters, and at
last safely in the dark.

Endings
Elizabeth W. Bennefeld

Lulled to sleep by weeping sands against the window,
mixed by winds with sleet and snow,
I dream again of golden, glorious clouds
racing before that one last towering storm—
the day the Earth last heard our voices,
felt our steps, and then
was washed by rains no more.

Exobiology II
F. J. Bergman

They waited until everyone on the planet
was able to pass a comprehensive test
before turning on the war machines.
The eradication parameters randomly
altered at 28-kilometer intervals, unless
low clouds intervened. Valuable artifacts
had been destroyed, but their most ordinary
objects (worn-out garden tools, old shoes,
blankets, erasers) were carefully arranged
in impregnable bunkers, with data pellets
containing a recording of every being
that had once been alive. They left us
no instructions on how to proceed.

Clotho Visits the Local Yarn Store
Paula Berman

Just once, I would like to spin sheep's wool.
I want to feel soft fibers in my fingers,
hold merino to my cheek in place of mortality.

I want to knit a warm sweater that hardly matters,
and if I drop a stitch, say "Oops! Oh well,
no one but I will ever notice that."

I want these chill hands to make scarves
only to warm me against mundane winds
—I want to create a gift of mere love
instead of the unasked favors of Fate.

Duty overmasters me: I am Destiny. I work
consequences rather than cashmere, spin
certainties, not silk. Sometimes, though—
my fingers yearn for fiber.

Godzilla's Better Half
Matt Betts

What is it about Tokyo that keeps you going back there time after time to
wreck it, to tear it down like you do? I want to understand, my darling
Gojira. Is it a hatred, a compulsion maybe? Do you wake from terrible
dreams with the city's name on your lips?

It was impressive when you leveled the town the first time, but when
you obliterate the same city over and over it looks like you're afraid to
try something new. Like you have no ambition. I believe in you, baby. It's
everyone else that needs to see what you can do.

Is there another woman that draws you in with your breath flaming, scales
atwitter? Is that it? Is the destruction all a cover-up—something to divert
attention from your indiscretion?

Does she make you so crazy you feel like knocking down a few buildings
just to show off? Is she the type that's impressed by a fleeing populace and
a stymied army?

I woke in the middle of the night and found you gone. The bed seemed so big without you there. When you came back you said you went jogging, but I could smell Tokyo on your clothes, your breath. I knew you were lying to me.

What is it about Tokyo? If it's not a big deal, take me with you next time and show me why you love it and hate it. Why you embrace it and push it away. Take me with you and we'll smash tanks and topple skyscrapers together.

Scent & Sensibility
Robert Borski

If it helps, perhaps the disbeliever
might try to think of perfume,
for there are many similar attributes
between the two.

Like invisibility. And sensitivity
to light.

Both often leave traces of their presence
behind, which include

not only a primary scent,
but undernotes of fear or sumptuousness,

the soul, atomized, like attar
or ambergris

or plucked with violence from
some field

(murder, of course, still makes
the best loam.)

Just open up the nares of
the mind and take a visual sniff.

Perhaps then you will allow
yourself to see the discorporium

with its many ghosts (death
has more than one

bouquet), some of

who would warn us, others
to take revenge—

or in my case make a final
fragrant goodbye

as,
breathless, you inhale me.

The Time Traveler Takes His Nth Lover at a Point of Departure
Bruce Boston and Marge Simon

Just as I'm leaving this time
I meet you waiting for a train.
You smell of soap and cheap cologne,

the kind kids buy for their mothers
and teachers at discount stores.
Beneath the scent, I sense your fear

like a ground swirl of bitter memory.
Was it his shadow before a midnight
window in the indivisible dark,

blotting out the hard white stars
and the limbs of leafless trees?
Was it what no longer happened

in your parents' bedroom that
entailed a childhood's end?
The train ratchets by with bars

of light for rich and poor alike.
You know what has transpired
in the hidden coaches, within

the walls of private cells,
the self of passive prisons.
Your scars give you away.

Centuries have come and gone
in the flash of a passing station
since my arrival in this era of

hidden passions and unspoken ties.
Take my hand and lie down with me
between these tracks that reach

to the event horizon and back again,
where even the death of an insect
can change the past forever.

Nine Views of the Oracle
Rachel Manija Brown

One

The oracle's house is built of bone and stone, of slim bamboo sticks and
stalks of yarrow. It's decorated with haunted dice and plaques inscribed
with desperate wishes.

Blue light flickers from the cracks in the walls. (The oracle has no need
of windows.) The oracle is inhaling the fumes from the sacred fires. The
oracle is watching NASDAQ.

The entrails fertilize her garden. Do not stray from the path.

Two

The oracle reads a book whose letters correspond to numbers. Each
formula reveals a different story.

If you sneak a peek while her back is turned, you will become convinced
that if you count the tendrils on the oldest banyan tree in the forest, mul-
tiply by the number of lizards in the desert, and divide by the number of
customers who enter your shop on the day of your birthday, you will find
the number of breaths remaining to you.

This never ends well.

Three

The oracle excels at math. The oracle speeds through the Sunday crossword. The oracle could have cracked the Enigma code in a day, but no one invited her to try.

The oracle never speaks without invitation.

Four

If your true love will die by your own right hand, do you really want to know?

Five

The oracle is not immortal. Some day she will search for another person —male or female, it doesn't matter, this is the oracle—who can meet her gaze without fear.

Their daughter will have eyes the color of heartbreak, and stars on the palms of her hands.

Six

The oracle's attendants have a word written across the soft clay of their foreheads. The oracle has a line of numbers tattooed across her arm.

Knowledge isn't always power.

Seven

You do not need to count the stanzas. Like the years of your life, the oracle counts for you.

Eight

The ninth stanza is the answer to your question. If you look long enough, you will understand.

Nine

Millennial Mass
G. O. Clark

On the altar
of a forgotten age

fragments of a contrail
and sonic boom subsided,

the flickering electronic glow
from an abandoned family room,

an old tin box full of universal
toy soldiers, broken in pieces,

a cracked tachometer,
pointer forever frozen in the red,

and the old Book of Law from a
religion long ago digitized,

all darkly blessed
by the silver skinned priest,

the future etched
in his stained glass eyes.

The Airships Take Us,
Even As We Blow Out The Last Candle
David Clink

1. Pitch-blackness comes on like a tarantula.

2. Goodnight, Mrs. Calabash, wherever you are.

3. The air is arctic against my skin
    with the scent and earshot of a bird in it.
    I can taste its reluctance to come near.
4. It tastes like my mother's old apron
    the day we put it in the kindled fireplace,

5. the day Samuel E. Danvers of Hatfield,
    Massachusetts, was committed
    to the Worcester Sanitarium 12 Mar 1873,
    age 42, of a brain disorder.

6. The darkness did not come on like a tarantula.
    It was always here.
7. It is penetrated by man-made machines
    muscling into the night,
8. by two young women on a downtown bus
    with blue streaks in their hair, whispering,
    "Calvary," and, "Hosanna."

9. Giantism in dinosaurs caused the world to tilt
    on its axis,
10. not to mention the recent watercooler gossip
    about the chemistry of love and fidelity.

11. The small hands of Time are holding
    the dark mirror of Vanity, saying with a glance:
    Look at yourself. Look at how others look at you.
    Remember when this didn't matter?
12. We were as happy as willows, then,
13. when we built an airship from spare parts
    and a kit. It took all night. We lifted off
    before the morning sneezed all over us.

14. Durwood remains in the bygone, a regret confined
    by memory, by a real or imagined happening.
15. Tomorrow he will try to learn from his past mistakes.

16. It is known in some circles as the "Great Dying":
    251 million years ago an extinction level event
    killed 96% of all marine species and an estimated
    70% of land species.
17. The ones that survived forgot the world
    was larger than the horizon.

18. Le gustaría acompañarnos al teatro?

19. When the darkling leaves our planet,
    it will be kind enough to turn off the lights,

20. even as the last men and women, dressed in
    Victorian attire, board the remaining airships,
    the moon disappearing behind their sails,
    even as their hulls kiss the tops of trees.

NOTES:
The poem is in a form defined by Jim Simmerman. It follows
his poetry writing exercise "Twenty Little Poetry Projects"
which can be found in the book titled *The Practice of Poetry* by
Robin Behn and Chase Twichell.

Line 2: Jimmy Durante used the phrase to sign off his radio
show in the 1940s.

Line 8: Calvary: the hill near Jerusalem where Jesus was crucified.
1 : an open-air representation of the crucifixion of Jesus
2 : an experience of usually intense mental suffering

Line 8: Hosanna: Middle English osanna, from Old English,
from Late Latin,
from Greek hōsanna, from Hebrew hōshī āh-nnā pray, save (us)!
—used as a cry of acclamation and adoration

Line 18: Would you like to go with us to the theatre?
leh goos-tah-REE-ah ah-kohm-pah-NYAHR-nohs ahl teh-AH-troh?
http://www.fodors.com/language/llresults.cfm?lid=1&cid=13

Outward, Through the Inner Worlds
Malcolm Deeley

Out of death, the journey from core to edge,
vast center, toward the night of giants.

1. Sol

He looked into the sun, watched the roar of atoms,
and when he turned away his eyes were white,
icy diamonds, and his profile was a vast eclipse.

2. Mercury

Forgotten, the sound of voices.
Instead, the peace of desires burned away.
Turn from the sun, look out.
Black falls into black, and blindness is welcome.
I have hurt too many, and now I want to touch
the surface of a sphere; seared and frozen, lifeless,
rolling, slave of the sun, which burns my back
as I pass the tortured face
of a child chained too close.

3. Venus

Moonless and seething with liquid heat.
I would like to lie on that ravaged surface;
feel the appalling pressure. Poison air, crushing.
I will stay until a vision of touching her
beneath the waves of an imagined sea
becomes the same as my presence,
spread-eagled, face up
under her blanket of chemical rain.

4. Earth

Blue eye, calling me to remembrance.
Blue eye, accuse me all you like.
I'll pass.
Red Death is next.

5. Mars

Brother to the House of Prospero.
Ruddy with age and silence.
You were alive once, wet, and fierce.
The winds still roar at your towering heights
and in the low places of your cracked skin.
Pounded with violence that bears no malice.
Then waiting, unhurried,
for the ancient scars to fade.

Edgar Allan Poe
Bryan D. Dietrich

Your Edgar Allan Poe action figure comes
wrapped in plastic, form fitting, vacuum
packed. You believe this makes him happy.
Each rubber wrist restraint, each cellophane
strip strapping a leg here, a shoulder there,
each breath breathed against the unforgiving
container makes it more like home. Your Edgar
Allan Poe action figure doesn't *do* anything.
He may be fully articulate, but never speaks.
His only accessory, a raven. No jet pack,
no Kung Fu grip. His slick hair won't grow
longer or shorter with the twist of a knob.
No pull-string to make him mope. This latter
comes natural. If you leave him long enough,
his head simply declines, chin and chest grow
intimate. It's not as if he wants to be this.
It's not even, really, a matter of choice.
Nor can one say he's sad. He was made
this way, pre-packaged. Or perhaps you only
assume, knowing what you know of poets.
It says it right here, on the back of the box,
weapon of choice: Morbid Rumination.

Apple Jack Tangles the Maidy Lac
with a Red, Red Ribbon
Amal El-Mohtar and Jessica Paige Wick

APPLE JACK: You're stubborn as the cleft in a goat's hoof
or bad living in the doctor's final report!
Come live with me by the apple-tree
and I'll brew you apple-jack. I'll stir
eggshell-stew in an old tin pan used,
once, to collect rain-water from a goldriver.
I'll even bake old-fashioned lavender-spice bread.
We can pretend the ribbon isn't wrapped around
our wrists, that our fingers aren't enlaced, if only
you'll say my name, you'll look at me, even once.
If only, even once, I could look away from you,
straying by the glassy pool.

MAIDY LAC: Egg-shell stew? Is that a joke?
A crackerjack box cruelty?
I'll never look at you, never,
wicked, tricking, tripping thing
with your cat's breath panting 'round my fingers
tugging me away. All I wanted was a ribbon,
a red, red ribbon for my wine-dark hair,
not an ugly gnarled apple-lad, limp-mouthed and dry.
Blast your apples, blast your trees
with sky-forks and sea-salt, blast them all!
My eyes are shut until I'm free
to sink beneath the wide lake's rim
and find my way back home.

APPLE JACK: Home's right through here. This door thick with thorn?
A ruse to keep away the rubes.
I want you to eat. Eat an apple at least.
Look at the tree, the copper brightness
of the fruit. Maybe we'll live forever.
Apple-trees wear a crown of blossom,
not lightning. Oh, please, shake off
the water's curse, don't thin off like wax
in the heat. Look at me, my soda-pop,
we needn't think of the ribbon at all,
just the latest radio tune, ghost stories,
Old Grandpappy in the Moon visiting.

MAIDY LAC: This ribbon's a tangle, not a knot,
and I'll slip free of it, see if I don't.
I don't want your apples, don't want your blossoms,
your copper and your thorns. I want
the waves, the warm kiss of depth and dream,
of dripping hair on my bare shoulders. It's cold out here, apple-man,
it's cold, and the wind is a knife on my flesh,
will peel me to my core. I won't go, I won't—but tell you what.
I'll stuff your mouth with weeds, I'll pull you down instead.
This ribbon tugs both ways, no?
My strength is not so small as my wrist,
and I've heard that apples float.

Joyride
Angel Favazza

As the jet car ignites
It emits greenish luminescent smoke
From its fiery steel exhaust.

With an electric murmur it gently hums
Along with a piano-string scurry
Across the orange clouds.

From my optical helmet,
I see them below like a swarm of steel fireflies
And with a three-thousand-foot swoop
I catch up.

My ear speaker-button warns of an angry
Parental Interstellar Regulations sighting.
They'll find us! They'll find us with their
Forward-rolling vessel and single-minded flight.

With a sudden trick of reflection and
A soundless explosion of violet dust
I fly like a scalded bird.

As I turn to look, hovering soundlessly
Next to me is the civilian babysitter's vessel.
Within a porthole the blinding glare of my mom,
Arms crossed, standing in her blue floral housecoat.

The Qin Golem
Francesca Forrest

After years in prison, so I'm told,
Zhao was freed and came to visit me
And the other eight thousand
Where we stood silent and forever ready
To fight our lord's wars in the afterworld.

What books he must have read
Or tales he must have heard
I cannot say,

But he jumped the red rope barrier,
And ran to me, an officer,
Took a knife to my forehead,
Inscribed me with 真理
Before they grabbed him.

Awakened, now I search for him.
I have broken the walls and bars of countless prisons
But I have not found him.
Their lead missiles have chipped my shoulders, hit my chest
But I have not fallen.

I have walked to the southern sea
And I have not found him.
How may I rest?
Waves wash by me and I kneel.
Will water wash away the word that waked me?
Can truth dissolve like clay?

Cities in Fog
Robert Frazier and Andrew Joron

in memory of Gene Van Troyer

today his internal suburbia is fetched with black rain
and wild hanging gardens frosted by albino crows

today her voice seems to calve to hundreds
its order carrying an arbitrary valence

today they cling to romantic artifice
their destiny as surgeons of the what-was

tomorrow they will map shattered portraits
and listen for the thoughts of their lost

mirror-images, scheduled to announce
their own identities in place of the real

meanwhile, a periphery of giant funnels
is moaning jazzoid into the night sky

there are streets that wind cycloid into
dead suns, scattered word-like upon light's whiteness

today there are windows that return the stares
of all witnesses to the crimes of the crystallizing eye

Rapunzel Considers the Desert
Jeannine Hall Gailey

Like learning a foreign language,
I want to learn
a new sand—hardscrabble and brown.
I want a new heat in my blood.
blinded and shorn,
I desire new fruit
grown under an unforgiving sun.
Prickly pear,
open yourself to me. Agave nectar.
Quail, jackrabbit,
grackle and green hummingbird,
let your shadows fall.
Let a fierce light try to turn me to dust.

Conjunctions
Neil Gaiman

Jupiter and Venus hung like grapes in the evening sky,
frozen and untwinkling.
You could have reached up and picked them.

And the trout swam.

Snow muffled the world, silenced the dog,
silenced the wind...

The man said, I can show you the trout. He was
glad of the company.
He reached into their tiny pool, rescued a dozen, one by one,
sorting and choosing,
dividing the sheep from the goats of them.

And this was the miracle of the fishes,
that they were beautiful. Even when clubbed and gutted,
insides glittering like jewels. See this? he said, the trout heart
pulsed like a ruby in his hand. The kids love this.
He put it down, and it kept beating.
The kids, they go wild for it.

He said, we feed the guts to the pigs. They're pets now,
They won't be killed. See? We saw,
huge as horses they loomed on the side of the hill.

And we walk through the world trailing trout hearts like dreams,
wondering if they imagine rivers, quiet summer days,
fat foolish flies that hover or sit for a moment too long.
We should set them free, our trout and our metaphors:

You don't have to hit me over the head with it.
This is where you get to spill your guts.
You killed in there, tonight.
He pulled her heart out. Look, you can see it there, still beating. He said,
See this? This is the bit the kids like best. This is what they come to see.

Just her heart, pulsing, on and on. It was so cold that night,
and the stars were all alone.
Just them and the moon in a luminous bruise of sky.

And this was the miracle of the fishes.

God's Cat
Lyn C. A. Gardner

Max believes the world is his field mouse
leaps straight onto my back while I'm standing straight,
as if I were his tree,
his claws digging in, secure
of his welcome,
chirping his plaintive commentary straight into my ear:
The ear of God, and he
my furry begotten son, sleek and dark as night,
bedeviling even my most privileged disciples
with his demands.
No demon's pointed tail is sacred.

No angel's wings can flutter past
without swift, targeted destruction,
torn to shreds and feathered shards like some common
garden-variety bird.
His irreverence is terrifying:
for me, my works, my favored ones—
as if by inviting him here
I've given all the affirmation he needs
to a one-beast reign of loving terror.
You should hear his furry chuckle
as he barrels down the hall
to slash your head—
just one quick fang to the neck—that's it—dig in—
it's good, isn't it,
viewing everything in the world
from up here on
God's shoulder.

—*with thanks to Brian Conn*

From Tindalos
Wade German

It's not a dream

You've been sleepwalking through
ancestral forests,
transplanted so long ago
on this terraformed moon.
And it would be Beltane
back on Earth, had it
not lost the strange temptation
to exist.

As the distant sun, blood-red
and nearly dead,
sinks behind Saturn's rim,
twilight comes with baleful howls of
hounds that hail not
from Annwyn's fairy realm,
but beyond time's angle
and the silent curvature of space.

And you know you can only wait
at this pre-established spot
among the trees,
where star-winds blow
ashes of extinguished worlds
through the dark, nebulous boughs
of your branching memory—
the source of psychic scent they seek
from Tindalos.

At Death's Door
Larry Hammer

Within the waste, dawn was diluted light
not yet tinged with colors other than shades
of black. Soon the sun's flood would stream high
above him, washing the bare world sere and pale
with the heat of desiccation, but for now,
small mercies, it was cool enough to walk

and bright enough to see where others had walked
before him—sunset drained away the light
to a dark unlike any he'd known till now,
no moon nor star, nothing to splash a shade.
He had been glad to rest, though. Taut and pale,
he stood, hiked his battered pack up high

on his shoulder, and continued on to the height
of the next slow rolling hill at a walk.
By the time he reached the ridge, the sky had paled
enough he could see the next had the same light
slope, the same thorn scrub, same lack of shade
as everywhere since the forest, and only now,

after countless stones and dry arroyos, now
he felt despair. After days of dearth in high
plains, after the Dark Wood with its angry shades,
what here drained all purpose from his vain walk?
He couldn't tell. He stared at the endless light,
at this uncrossable wasteland of Death's Pale

until he saw them: four buildings of pale
adobe in the wash below, visible now
that he knew where to look within the light
landscape. He hadn't expected this—a high
tower perhaps, with walls on which guards walked
to keep apart the living and dead shades.

Sun poured in his face, forcing him to shade
his eyes with a gaunt hand. Below, his pale
wife waited, the lodestone of his walk,
his be-all end, his life. It was time now
to do what he had once set out with high
purpose to do but seemed, in this alien light,

a shade of wish: fetch her. But how? Well, now
he must. Before the pale sun surged high
he walked to Death's Hall under its flowing light.

Parental Pride
Carolyn M. Hinderliter

parental pride
so white, so sharp
baby's first fangs...
a perfect pair
for every mouth

hillbilly invasion
David C. Kopaska-Merkel

I'm sorry, Darlene,

the alien nano I picked up on Io
has messed me up sumthin fierce:
built a data warehouse in my head
so I'm recording this;
you're ovulating and
I made sure the pills won't work no more.
And the baby?
You don't wanna know.

Fungi From Yuggoth
Michael Kriesel

Zemo, Hell's Baron, face always ablaze.
Yellow flames licking his head finally
extinguished. Decapitation. An ax
wielded by Doctor Strange, arch mage. One blow.
Vital lesson comics taught me at twelve:
ugly things occur in the occult. You
try a spell anyway. Nothing, at first.
Still, the back of the neck knows better, as
random acts begin. Lightning rod, the air
quiets all around me. A Suzy-Q
plops on the table at lunch. I look up.
Overhead, a hole in the air leads to
nowhere. I long for normalcy's return.
Mechanistic universe. Start to om.
Lovecraftian blue tentacles plug all
kitchen sink drains. Strangle the cat. Attack
just as I'm flushing a stale PBJ.
It's enough to make you pray. Almost. I
hear the abyss howl behind the wall. Tough
guy, I make a deal with some crabs that wing
freely across the interstellar gulf,
Earth to Yuggoth in two days. My brain's here,
dangling from a giant claw, in a sealed
can with speakers, lens, though I can't lip-sync—
but better the devil you know—like Bob,
a great guy, my ride across the void's sea.

Earthrise, Viewed from Meridiani, Sol 687
Geoffrey A. Landis

A blue-white speck,
fuzzy through gauzy grey clouds,
rising over pale yellow dunes
in a pale pale sky
while cosmic rays flicker like fireflies at the edges of vision.

That's you
and me
and everybody you know;

everyone who ever lived,
everyone who ever died.
All of us.

Were you smiling? Did you wave?

Finding the God Particle
Sandra Lindow

*Without...God particles, "atoms would have no integrity, so there would be
no chemical bonding, no stable structures—no liquids or solids—and, of
course no physicists and no reporters."*
                    —Stephen Fried, "The Race for the Secret of the Universe"

It is something and nothing,
the God particle;
everything else is mass:
tables, chairs and books,
the lint we remove from dryer filters,
even the air we breathe.

But the God particle
is like the matrix of a poem,
invisible force,
slowing what is born
massless at light speed,
pulling, binding the words together
until it takes form.

We cannot see where it begins
only the words of where it's been:
the subatomics of creation,
colliding in darkness,
taking shape in the ashes
of beauty, desire and pain.

At Fermi Lab
scientists find the secret
of universal cohesion,
not in their particle accelerator:
but in their luminous dreams.

Layers of Man
John C. Mannone

After Layers of Man, Expressionism
Mixed media on paper by Jason Carusillo

Sometimes everything is black and white with symmetry of good and evil.
Like the hypocrites in the Gospels of Matthew and Dr. Luke, each a
casket, smooth mahogany white, yet full of dead man's bones—the living
dead—skin peeled off the charcoaled face, sinew frayed, off-gray. Cut
away the milk-colored, yet soured, yellow-looking flesh, to the pure bone
white frame caging a black heart—the beauty of hatred.

Alexander von Humboldt Visits the Moon
Sharon Mock

He comes to the New World
to make his name. Instead
his name makes him. He writes
and syllables scatter, lifted
like *Platanus* seeds by the wind.
His progeny take root
miles past where his feet step.
When he bathes in the ocean
long red schools upwell
to feed on stray letters
washed off in the tide.

One night, as he sleeps
in a tent by the river,
the Moon comes in the shape
of a woman, pale and austere.
She pulls him reluctant
over the treetops, through the ice
fiber of cloud, for a better view.

She is neither silver nor cheese
but basalt underfoot,
comfortable stone. His feet
leave no mark in the dust.
On the horizon, a lazurite bead
dangles blinding, bright,

beyond his reach. From here
every pattern shows distinct,
complexity condensed,
flattened to surface and line.

The Moon's light hand
holds a palmful of dust to his face.
In its eddies, lines of men
launch upward, driven by water
and engineering, driven by the will
of politics and exploration.
They leave footprints and flags
but their names drown
beneath the sea *america*, none of them
as potent as his own.

He awakens, cold and clean-footed,
as the moon sinks behind
the forest canopy. A diamond winks
from dark shadow and is gone.
He tells nobody what he has seen.

But the astronomers know.

Triangulation
George Moore

for Sherri Smith and Donna Dewhurst Nordstrom

When word reaches me
I walk outside
and stare hard at the night sky
the blackbirds have taken
the late spring snow as confusion
the Great Salt Lake
shimmers in its white emptiness
and the stars seem to challenge
that hamstrung sense of grief
her absence in the vacuum
that surrounds us.

In the cul de sac
the pastel homes are blind
and monotone, your son's
fifth birthday comes
and goes while you smoke a cigarette
sucking oxygen from a tube
outside the hospital doors.

There's much we do not know
what happens beyond the event horizon
where gravity becomes so strong
the world so small
but when she disappeared
you let the sky go truly black
as in the aftermath of a catastrophe
sucking up everything we might
have called light into an orbit
we could not escape.

Your cells went wild
in some kind of strange sympathy
as she drove off sleepily, silently
into the warp of the Snake
at Hell's Canyon.

I sat with your son
and we wished the birds away
watched them scatter across
the snow fields like inverse stars
on a polar shield, the first fledgling
greens smothered in the sky's late fury
and unfolded the night's texture
its just visible pinpricks
in our concurrent imagination
hungry beyond belief for the next sign
of some planetary fraternity.

Conrad, in the Autopsy Room
Kristine Ong Muslim

When they finally cut him up, they noticed that
the flesh underneath was like sugared sun.
It was like what Grampa said: *We were all yellow inside.*
That wrong shade of yellow—the color of the gods.
Conrad was only pretending to be dead.
He liked the attention humans give to dead bodies.
Must have amused him to wallow in their confusion
while they tear up his insides and find that it was all
yellow goo. No organs. Just bones and that small
round mass inside his ribcage—his new head to replace
the old one next year. It's our peculiar way of *molting.*
One of them curiously poked at Conrad's miniature head
growing inside his chest. It was still malformed, still
in the early stages of development. The head had tiny
pinpricks of eyes which would not close, eyelashes still absent.
Only one of the medical examiner's assistants screamed.
The other rushed out of the room.
From Conrad's mouth poured forth honey
then a swarm of black flies.
Conrad was home an hour later
and laughingly told us what happened.

The Tree of Forgiveness
Kristine Ong Muslim

This was the orchard where all myths started.
A man and a woman, the keeper hissed,
both prowlers. They were searching for the
North Star. I told them that there was
no such thing as North, let alone a star by that
name; directions were invented to confuse.

The woman wept, could not believe how they
were fooled. Furious, the man swatted, thrashed
an overhanging branch where apple blossoms
rustled their secrets. The keeper tore off his mask,
smiled, told them: "There is no Other. I am One."
The man nodded in agreement. The woman gathered

her skirt of flowers and small bones crackling
as if it were made of dried leaves being trod upon.
"You lie," she accused. She was so beautiful;
the keeper tried hard not to fall in love. "No, madam.
If you have read the travel book carefully, then you
will notice the implications of the tree cited there,"

the keeper explained, his tone polite, his newly molted
skin discreetly hidden where shadows could not even
reach. The man wanted to stay, asked if he could work
in the orchard. "Absolutely," said the keeper, satisfied,
imagined the man tending the tree where the worms grew.
"It would be a pleasure." The keeper was an honorable man;

he believed in choices. The woman moved on, down where
the green oceans thrived and the mountains were born.
The man did not ask her to stay with him. Perhaps, the love
between them disappeared a long time ago when he gave her
the charge of carrying a child. Saddled by the weight of her
garments, she took them off. And the keeper swallowed hard.

Apsara
Shweta Narayan

I. Among the Seelie

She sings the orphaned river's plaint
to monsoon winds and thunderhead mothers
and they laugh.
Their songs have tones tones semitones
and different seasons.

Like you stepped on a cat

She slices her tongue in half to sing
their tones tones semitones
hides with them from cars and church bells
sheds sandalwood for oak
plants silence

Pakkiepakkiepakkie
Serve your betters

She runs to Sidhe arms thorn-strong petal-soft
and white
To clear-brook music that quenches enchants
envelops her

He finds her exotic.

II. Among the Devas

She sings in tones tones semitones,
dances different rhythms
and they laugh

Their tongues are broken in foreign or what?

She weeps for captive djinni
naked begging stark-eyed children
and the Taj.
Her grief rimes the court with salt and silence.

You don't like it here?
Then go.

She learns again the taste of amrit
more bitter than her memory
and monsoon's first warm tears
more sweet

III. Exile

Where Kitsune and Anansi
are strangers together
she is not strange

She can wear eucalyptus redwood coconut
sing in tones tones ragas
She can—*takita taka dhimi*—
dance.

But when monsoon is a memory
and dust wind dries her voice away
she listens

alone
for Coyote's sobbing giggle

And he laughs.

The Bears Are Working
Shweta Narayan

While you dream, the bears are working.
Snowbear paints your inner glade;
Stormbear roars the monsters, lurking
deep in Treebear shade.

When you run from claws and shadows,
raise the drawbridge, shut the keep,
Leafbear rustles shushing murmurs
till you dream of sleep.

While you dream, and dream of dreaming,
Stonebear melts your walls away.
Starbear limns the moondark self
you cower from by day.

Particles and Planets
James B. Nicola

I, too, obey the law of gravity:
On every passing person I exert
some force, as every person does on me,
like particles and planets. To avert
disaster, those insensate drifters veer
respectfully, through either outer space
or inner, and continue to career
unbruised. Likewise behaves the human race,
year after year, though every pulsing heart
that bustles down Fifth Avenue at noon
is pulled by others at it spins apart
in its own distant orbit, like a moon.
Some think this separateness a sort of pride;
I think of it as care, lest we collide.

It Snowed
Mark Rich

It snowed the day the world died
the world over
I mean it snowed the world over
dry sand deserts now chill and covered
lakes ice-stilled and now snow-blanketed
even oceans sloshing to a stop
great tidal bulging stillnesses
thickly rolling with wind-waving white
snow a thousand feet thick
at the bottom of gaping open-strip mines
seeping into the deepest elevator shafts
in sleet-silenced Manhattan
thick and blinding upon jungle-stripped hillsides
still deepening over nearly invisible
Matterhorns
volcanoes the only steaming battles left—
mist against snowfall—
and the people covered in snow
—   there being still people—
never thought to reach for shovels
their grandparents made
and stored against such a day
for people had forgotten how to do things
for themselves, forgotten
how to use their own hands
forgotten, I say
which is what I mean by saying
the world died.

Nonrenewable Resources
Marsheila Rockwell

The oil and coal are gone
Natural gas, too
Weather has become so unpredictable
And violent
That wind and wave are no longer options
And no one remembers when we last saw the sun
But the human race powers on

Harnessing the energy of creative minds—
Poets, writers, musicians, artists
Interior decorators and chefs
Even my old gardener, Milt—
Strapping them into machines
That turn the neurons which once fired
Their imaginations
Into utilitarian electricity
Lighting a multitude of identical grey cities,
Running billions of identical grey cars,
And raising vast beds of bland grey algae to feed
A population that grows even blander
With every passing synapse

Of Amaranth and Honey
Marsheila Rockwell

Once they worshiped me

Their left-handed hummingbird

God of fire, of war
Feeding me from sunrise altars
Their hearts, their blood, their youth

Then the white lords came
Bearing disease on six legs
And they turned from me
To kneel before a wooden cross
And a brown-faced virgin

Now, unremembered

I am an old man watching

Telenovelas

Eating cheap salsa and low-fat

Tortillas from a bag

Laments of the Lucid Dreamer
Charles Saplak

1

Learn early how all wonders occur as one sleeps—fat,
florid elf decides what toys you need; mystic rabbit sneaks
in to lay chocolate-crème eggs; glimmering fairy plucks
kid seeds, baby teeth, from beneath your pillow.

2

Succubi introduce golden youths one by one, wetly, to adult
pleasures, yet never stay behind to help to hide the shame.

3

The US Air Force, one night in basic training, implanted a
microchip beneath my skin. It itched when I awoke. Years
later, it still records my movements, tracks all my cash
and credit purchases, and "e-mails" anonymous and false
accusations to prospective employers. How else to explain?

4

Nightmare, goblin of face, long of fang, worm of tongue,
rides skeletal horse 'round and 'round rills of my mind.

5

Burglars occasionally sneak in; point weapons at my
pillowed head, laugh at my meager excuses for treasure,
read my mail, sneak out again after hiding my eyeglasses.
Sensing their presence, I send desperate yet unheeded
commands to my hands to slap my own face, to my mouth to
yell loud enough to awaken me.

6

Sleep: dark skin of ocean's face, unimaginable sharks
gliding nearby, unseen, on other side.

7

One of every three hundred surgery victims in America is
incompletely anaesthetized, remaining fully conscious but
paralyzed throughout all procedures. I am one of these.

8

One summer night, Greys and Reptilians, in a rare display
of extraterrestrial cooperation, creep into my rural home,
clamp thought disruptors to my brain stem, walk me out with
a handheld tractor beam. 2001 tests are run, with
unimaginable probes and wires. I glimpse reflections of
Zeta Reticuli, but never receive test results in the mail.

9
Each Lover inevitably creeps outside as I doze too deeply,
takes other lovers, forgets me, pursues alternate careers.
10
Oh, to read the obituary, to hear the eulogy, to mingle
amongst the long-lost friends and family who could never
until now find the time—but no. Just dissolve, become
muddied, lie still, and measure the depth of the darkness.

To Theia
Ann K. Schwader

> *Theia, a hypothetical protoplanet, is central to the*
> *Great Impact Theory of the Moon's origin.*

That you were our meant earth, & not this other
flawed marble we crawl over, cling to, dream
in fits of leaving—surely this suspicion
once wove Atlantis through us, carved out Eden
between our ribs.

That we are shattered creatures,
our sacred texts assure us, but not why
the iron that marks our blood is restless, seeking
some heart beyond our hearts.

No second impact
remains to reunite our cores: Lagrange
holds only pebbled mercies, shooting stars
not worth the wishing on.

Come summer midnights
when song dogs serenade your final shard,
we cannot help but raise our faces also
to that remotest of reflected blessings
& howl you, Theia, as the home we lost.

Two Kinds of Time
Meliors Simms

In some universes
time is experienced as linear.
Individuals move through their lives
cutting a track into their possibilities
and paving it into permanence behind them.
Aware only of the winding road they have chosen,
looking backwards down the line from now to birth
looking forward into the obscure thicket of the future
sometimes, peripherally aware of a bare hint
of what ifs as what isn't.

In some universes
time is experienced as a plane.
Beings move around their existence
as an intimate landscape
treading and retreading every possibility.
Learning their lives as a gardener learns her land,
choosing every choice
exploring every opening,
until through preference
a rut is worn in the familiar
a dwelling in just one favourite moment or cycle of moments
a resting place from their endless wanderings.

When you sleep
these universes meet in your dreams.
Time leaks across the boundaries
so you can know a little
of the strange ways of linearity or planearity;
whichever is most unfamiliar to you.

For a Few Coins, I Draw You a Picture
Marge Simon

Antoine creates promising statues in basalt. All of them are big women
with tiny breasts.

Nobody wants to buy his statues, but the townsfolk love him. When
the earth moves, we know Antoine has finished another statue of a big

woman with tiny breasts. Antoine has a model for this. He uses her over and over. Sometimes he sculpts her eating a small aircraft. Antoine's largest statue is in the town square.

My sister Celeste is crazy about the paintings of Archimboldo. She makes busts of dictators from rotting vegetables and crusts of leftover sandwiches. Most of them look like our mayor, Mr. Modine. Celeste doesn't like criticism.

For a few coins, I draw you a picture. When I make the picture, you will love it. I make the picture on the sidewalk, see? Such a pretty woman, a fine face. Strong jaw, but still sweet. It is okay, no? Hand me your purse, trust me. I will create this work from your own palette. Here is your lipstick, right? Okay. I use this for your mouth. Such a beautiful mouth, there. Now it is in the cement. So, back to your purse. And what have we here? Your personal blush to match the lovely flowers of your cheeks, like so. Ah! now we find the rest of your face, hiding so coyly behind your pretty handkerchief. It's only a used tissue, but we don't care, do we? Two coins for your glowing brown eyes. Voila! So. There you are, most beautiful woman. There is your image on the cement for all to admire!

The Changeling Always Wins
Nicole Kornher-Stace

It will not eat. It will not sleep.
It climbs the walls and spits at me.
It is no child: only from afar
will those hands, those eyes,
that grin pass for innocent.
It is weeping like a hangman's daughter.
It is wailing like a fiddle at a demon's chin.
It is laughing like old ice trod underfoot.
It is vomiting warm curds on my new shoes.
It is pulling all my bookmarks out.
It is gumming the coals from my hearth.
I don't care what you say.
It is no child.
Oh, how I hate the town wives
with their households like a sampler verse:
my children are lovely, my children are good;
my children always do just as they should
while it babbles in its argot like thieves-cant,

the gabblish tongue of twins,
and watches me sidelong, and slaps
my ass, and sinks
its needle teeth into my tit.
What would you have me do?
Heed the stories, thrash it till it squeals and—
what? Scrabbles out a map for me,
a lay of hills and greenwood, with an X,
long fingers spidered in the ash?
(Crow-child, fox-child, as if you would not lie.)
Trick it? Trick it? Its very heart pumps guile.
It is sly as sharks in shipwrecks, slick as
Death gone courting. Me, I'd sooner trick a stone.
Cut it open, turn its insides out?
What would I find?
A clockwork heart, a clot of earth,
a vein-fine plait of baby hair tied thrice,
which I might recognize?
(The long knives whisper darkly in their block.)
It rails at me like a jilted ghost.
(I sharpen them.)
It smiles at me like fever breaking.
(I let them rust.)

Cabaret
J. E. Stanley

No be-bop, no swing,
just the blues, slow blues.
That's all they want.
That's all we play.

What do these aliens feel
when they close their eyes,
sway slowly to human music?

Before their dinner,
I pop a couple black market judies,
washed down with imitation bourbon.
When they kick in, I close my own eyes,
visualize a different time,
playing Le Cercle Rouge back in New Chicago,

my horn floating over Tony's bass riff
and Amy's inverted chords.

After the show,
the guards lock us up in our small rooms.
I dream of aliens,
bug-eyed with sharp yellow teeth.
No judies at night.
I have to save those for the stage (And no,
I won't share the unspeakable things
I do to get them).

The next night, they bring us back out
through the kitchen, always
through the kitchen,
past that night's dinner:
women, children first.
Their dumb eyes, tear-stained,
plead silently.

And every night,
the manager comes up to the stage,
nods back toward the kitchen,
sneers and says,
"You boys better play well tonight."

City of Bridges
J. E. Stanley

I am the Keeper of Bridges
in the City of Bridges.
The Travelers always ask
where the bridge will take them.
I tell them Heaven;
I tell them Hell;
I tell them the Void
and there's no turning back.
I always lie.
They always believe.

If it's late October
and the snow falls early,

I might tell them that the bridge
will take them to May
and the first breath of spring.
I will say that it's a long walk,
but in the middle there's a diner
with pie and coffee,
shelter and cigarettes.

I may promise that the world
of their dreams lies on the other side
but that the journey will change them
and their dreams will lose all meaning.

If it is a lost child, I might say,
"The bridge will take you home."

I never reveal the truth:
that this is the City of Bridges
where Bridge
leads to Bridge
leads to Bridge...

A Tale of Three Worlds
David Lee Summers

A river cuts through layers of rock.
No grass, no bushes, no trees anywhere.
The bare ground shuns the sun's caress.
The river stops cold at the poles.
A world without forests—Mars.

Purple hills roll toward the horizon.
Carbon dioxide bound up in the rock.
The terrain is a lover, enveloping sunlight.
There is a great sigh of carbon dioxide.
A world with acid rain—Venus.

A river cuts through layers of rock.
Purple hills roll toward the horizon.
Sunlight's touch is comfortable, familiar.
Human voyeurs intercede.
Cut down forests.

Release carbon dioxide.
A world in danger—Earth.

On Its Own
Anna Sykora

When humankind departed, irate, for parts unknown,
The planetary enterprise continued on its own,

Providing kinder species housing they require
In what may stand of trees on land, like islands in the fire.

The sun rolled back and forth again as day resumed its size;
The moon refused to note the loss of moody lovers' eyes;

A shaggy comet tossed its tail and fizzled golden-green
While galaxies, receding, looked the same unseen.

The Chymical Marriage
Sonya Taaffe

They belong dead, but we resurrect them
in silver nitrate and the feverish flicker
that dreams beat against the inner eye,
the yearning golem, his disdainful mate,
the alchemist as eccentric and involute
as his flasks and alembics proposing
a toast in gin like white mercury,
the shadow stitchery of Paracelsus
and Prometheus' fire. Like cornerstone
shades, they seep beneath our century,
the lyke-wake wedding, lightning-engraved,
the dragonseed breeding of current and bone
that gendered only ghosts, replicant echoes
in red earth and Tesla coils, a shy chemist
who once saved me a sunflower to pluck.
To all the ways we strive and multiply,
to creation, to the divine and monstrous,
the scientific world and all its hauntings
black and white: l'chaim. It is our only...

Owner's Manual:
Containing General Information on How to Use Your Brand New, State of the Art, Pure Bred, Happy Hosts Human Body
Marcie Lynn Tentchoff

Step one: Insert tentacle A1 into orifice A
(as shown in diagram 1)

Step two: Squirm strongly, in a distinct
counterclockwise motion until:
a) A1 is deeply rooted in A, and
b) Host has turned a cheery shade of blue.

Step three: Thrust roots down tube X
(marked with a dotted line)

Step four: With your core now firmly rooted,
draw in all remaining body parts through
orifice A, allowing any overhang to poke
out through orifices B, C, and D.

Step five: Position your sensory appendages
behind orbs L and M.

Step six: Enjoy your new viewpoint on the world,
courtesy of Happy Hosts Human Bodies!

Step seven: Be sure to tell all your friends
about your wonderful new host!

Trouble Shooting Note: Should your Happy Hosts
Human Body fail to satisfy your every
hosting desire, please feel free to disengage
(reverse steps one through seven)
and use the Happy Hosts Ecstatic Euthanasia Gun,
thoughtfully included with your purchase.

The Bookseller's Tale
Marcie Lynn Tentchoff

I let her read the stock, you know,
back when the slush of wintertime
pooled grey and filthy on the curb.
She'd slink in, shivering, from the street,
and page through books she couldn't buy,
her starved eyes opening in two O—
shaped doorways to their other worlds.

I didn't mind—her hands were clean,
and customers those days were few.
My shop was warm, and she was cold,
and hey, she really loved to read—
the stories seemed to fill her up,
to nourish her on hopes and dreams,
perhaps in place of food and love.
Hmm? No, I never learned her name—
it's not my place to ask too much.
But when I started noticing
that all the books she read would fade
to covers binding empty page
to empty page, I had to change
my policy, and bid her go.

But just the other day, you know,
I saw her passing by the store,
through red-gold drifts of Autumn leaves,
her belly swelling through her clothes.
And when I think of all the tales
she fattened on in wintertime,
I wonder what she nurtures there.

The Men All Pause
(a poem on Global Warming)
Stephen M. Wilson

In the autumn
of her life

Mother
Earth

has
one
final

MONUMENTAL

Hot-
flash.

Self-Portrait as Dryad, No. 7

Marly Youmans

The golden haze around these whips of limbs
Is glistening, awakening to light
Within retreating clouds—embattled fire
That melts the snow and pellmell sends the sky
To run in ditches near the highway's edge.

My God, I am no witch to suffer so—
Who tied me to this stake that frosts my skin?
Who makes me tremble with his solar heat?
Who takes my voice and shakes the syllables
Until I speak in otherworldly tongues?

Dear Christ, the world is aching in its grave,
And can I bear another spring-time thaw?
O Willow, Willow, I uncurl to let
The bite and simmer of this raking gold
Explode in leaves—green eyes that weep for me,
My harrowed hell, my star-enkindled tree.

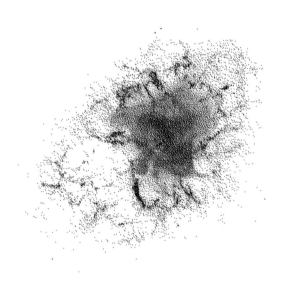

The Glass Ship
Mary Alexandra Agner

The ship wakes me and I must move
from a hundred years of sleep
through grogginess and my own hate of morning
right to red alert. I am not the first
the ship should call, there's other folks
more suited to hostiles in space,
astrogation, the paradox of parallax,
those lonely-night decisions command
has willingly taken up like oxen.
My specialty is good dirt and dowsing,
exploration on foot, immediate encounters
on a timescale far too fast
for image processing and spying satellites.
Blinking away tears, rubbing dried sleep
from my eyes, I see the emptiness
about me: every cocoon is quiet, burst
open, inhabitants let out to do their work.
I am the last, legs unsteady as I step down.
I wish for voices. There is the steady hum
of the ventilators, the only sound the ship
should ever make when all is well.
So all is well: no one to greet me,
the emptiness extending as I walk the halls
to medbay, where the bodies' smell
outpaces what recyclers can do.
No blood, no hurry, if I knew anything
of medicine beyond first aid, I'd say
that this was epidemic. The preparations clear
in the ordered equipment, anatomic scans blinking
from medical screens. I read the jargon
entered by the head doctor, old lover once
after the crew was picked, before we headed out.
Her face, turned sideways as in sleep,
exhausted, hollow, saliva crystallized
leaking a line down from her mouth,
the urgency of intimacy

reminding me of terror in a way the stench does not.
I cry to the ship's computer: "Report!"
and it rolls out its monotone
beginning with the date we left the dock.
I would let myself be caught up in past times,
a new solar system here, the images of nebulae
we passed, but for my lover's open eyes.
I swallow, swallow, both past and fear,
and bark back at the ship
for the last few days, for this disease.
I make to tell it I have clearance
but when it does not ask I realize
that it will tell me everything it knows
because there is no one to gainsay it,
no one of higher rank or politics
alive. It took them quickly
and like the horror stories, they did not progress
far enough before their deaths for a vaccine
or even an understanding. The ship is silent
in its own reproach. I find I'm staring
at those open eyes and the chicken skin
begins at the back of my neck and works downward.
Am I infected? I ask the ship
to lead me through the tests that tell me so.
Shaking, I walk up to the bridge, for I want to see
this particular blackness where I will die.
Ports open, swelled, staring: beneath me
is a blue-green swirl with a shawl of clouds.

My hunger—quick pain in my gut that flashes panic
before its common reason reaches my reason—
pulls me from the picture. Does it matter
to eat? But I do, take something stashed
in the snack compartments near communications.
As I swallow, I see the flashing lights
understood from my training days:
incoming communication.
Which switch? Which switch? My adrenaline
bombards my logic as my pulse goes up.
With a strangled sigh, I ask the ship
to answer, to let me speak.
The on-screen marble fades to black
and a small creature appears, short white beard,

overly rounded ears, almost-human face, movement
behind his back, shiny instruments and panels
like my own ship's center of command.
His eyes widen. What must I look like,
half dead with newly being alive,
limp bodies slumped over consoles as backdrop?
But he clears his throat and speaks.
I understand him. I make to reply and stop
myself, remind myself that I should be amazed
that his language is something I could know.
I get as far as "Greetings," quizzically I think,
before he cuts me off with a summary
of how they puzzled out my ship's warning.
I'm at a loss. He asks about the epidemic
and I send over all we learned. To my shock,
he smiles. His medmen have assured him
they are immune to our catastrophe.
They're here to study the planet
and so it seems, were we. Am I.
Would I like to join them when they descend?
The digits descending on my uniform's left wrist
tell me how many seconds left of life I have.
Their risk, I think, because how can I not
risk my last few days on a brand new world?

Composition of the atmosphere, compatibility
of life, all issues I let the computer chew on.
I do not care: there will be a wind
and we will set down by a stream
and if a single drop of spray or a breeze
kills me, what of it? I will have stood
and smelled and breathed deep of another world.
Six men land with the captain, shorter,
I find, than me, armed with pick axe
and pry tool: miners, they tell me,
who enjoy their work the old fasioned way.
We climb and trample and test and sample
for two days and I learn to know them well:
the one who falls asleep each chance he can,
one shy, one always angry, one allergic
to this splendid new place, eyes watering
and sneezing, a talkative near-optimist,
and one who speaks in actions rather than in words.

The captain, in his spectacles—*spectacles*
I laugh each time I see them wink in this new sunlight—
is kind, asking me about my past
(recording it; somehow he thinks I do not see
him thumb the switch on as he walks my way).
I fill notebooks with sketches, I watch insects
flit and land, I watch the local fish
grab the unwary from the water's top.
Here, I could have seen old lovers dance,
buildings go up by hand and then by crane,
listened to this deer-sized creature's hide
resound as drum. Instead, they dance for me,
each night as enormity comes down like stars.
On the third day, the coughing, the weariness,
and I watch as they begin to heat their forge
and fuse glass out of the nearby beach.
Great sheet after sheet, taller indeed than they,
glisten as I rest. The captain promises
that I will shine as a star in orbit,
a glass casket, space-worthy, circling
this new world. They want to name it after me.
And so, when they ask, I tell them: my mother
named me for a delight she'd never seen:
the pure, cold, white snow.

Rattlebox III
Mike Allen, Kendall Evans, & David C. Kopaska-Merkel

WITHIN THE BOX

Skinner's daughter is or is not
within the box, a paradox.
Is she learning an algebraic maze?
Programmed with rewards that come
When she turns the gum-machine knob?
Bowing and bobbing repeatedly, inexplicably,
As if praying to an idol?
Is she alive or dead, or
In some meditative, existential state
Somewhere inbetween?
Is it a Skinner or a Schroedinger box?

Or is it Jack who is or is not in there,
While we

OUTSIDE THE BOX

Crank the crank madly to deter-
mine his state,
Listening to the song about
Going 'round the mulberry bush
Or Robin's proverbial barn,
Can you hear the weasel popping?
Of course not!
If any information escapes the box
The waveform collapses
And whoever comes to be inside
If anyone, will know

THINK INSIDE THE BOX

Make no sense of these
thoughtforms
Flickering from this being's brain
Electrified in its own mazemind
That might be Skinner's daughter
Might be Jill or might be Jack
Climbing the beanstalk down the
Gravity well that's a mere pore on an
Asexual god's n-dimensional skin
In its multiple mind they go there
But don't they know

BEYOND THE BOX

It's terribly important
To not lose sight
Of the real questions
The important question
Is not whether Pandora or Rapunzel
Or Sleeping Beauty
Is still in the box
Ever was in the box
Clings to life
Inside the box.

BREAK THE GLASS

Holy crap, there may be no box
But how do you know?
What might you become
When the waveform collapses?
And if the box is never opened
Can you get to what matters?
Even so? Or maybe
All that matters is to

In one version
She's been sealed inside that box since
Before Big Bad Bang
Though how she got in there
That's a whole 'nother when, even
A whole 'nother (kind of) matter (or anti-matter)
And what you need to do
To spring her is to

BEYOND THE COSMOS

Let your eyes be fragmented
As your vision clears through higher
dimensions
Then no box is closed to you
Reach in, grab a fistful of anything
Whole universe your Halloween
candy bag
But! What! Is this?
Go to rescue your ageless sexless
gorgeous
Jilljack and you find four corners
And no way in!
And so you

Pick up the box and rattle it,
Like one of those Christmas presents
Hidden away on the top shelf
Behind your mom's hatboxes
Or beneath shoeboxes
In the closet bottom or
Beneath the basement stairs
Or beyond the heavy brass-bound door.

Rattle it a moment or two
And you are convinced, by the distinctive sound
It contains a time machine.
You open the box, climb inside,
And travel back to confront Skinner
Ask him why he locked his daughter
In the Box. He punches your light out,
The time-travel paradox subsequently

BREAKING ALL WAVE FRONTS SIMULTANEOUSLY

So are you going to open it?   The wave collapses.
                                                          Or it doesn't.

Rampage
John Amen

Von welcher mythischen Stadt begrüßt dasein?

i.

Mind
fortifies what it wishes to dismantle,
bogs itself in what it strives to transcend.

Its petals are pinned against yellow pages.

Mind
is scaling a graphic loop of rungs,
treading a bottomless conspiracy.

It has pressed the play button again.

Mind,
it crumbles in my fingers:

Encounter, react, systematize:

Je crée l'illusion; donc, je suis.

ii.

My neighbor's blood is viscous with envy.
His lawn trumps my daffodil bed;
my dreams putrefy in his wheelbarrow;
my defeats fertilize his manic bougainvillea.

I sit with vulgar people.
I stand with vulgar people.[1]

I forgot we'd be passing through Basel. Stop for a bite?
I hear your daughter took a casino job in east Thebes.
Congratulations on the summer home off Lake Cocytus.

---

[1] *I Ching,* Section 41 (Suen)

I'll forward you that stock tip as soon as I get home.
It's a sure thing, from Hector, my plastic surgeon friend,
the one who invested in Halliburton in the early days.

iii.

The suburb sprawls, its vinyl jaw unhinged,
raccoons, possums mangled on the highway.

Icecaps thaw, glaciers melt, polar bears drown
in the shelfless waters. Dumpsters in the Antarctic.

The maestros of petrol wave their batons,
sodomizing the great mother, siphoning her milk.

Mutant fungi in the crawlspace, stealth of bacteria.
The canyons weep, inauguration of murder.

True, poor Edomite, man is born unto trouble,[2]
but must we really give shelter to our betrayers?[3]

iv.

Dismissive snorts,
suspicious eyes, the clammy handshake.

Melancholy mannequins,
lipstick smiles carved into styrofoam faces.
Children in camouflage. The gloved hand
always scrawling in the black pad.

Silver cord of man, frayed and flapping in a sulfurous breeze.
President, Chairman, Emperor, Fuhrer,
still the locks on our kingdoms are made of greed and illusion.

Evening falls, fringed with barbed wire.[4]
Monks and dissidents vanish in the zyklon night.

---

[2] *Job* 5:7
[3] *Greek Myths* (Graves), section on "The Epigoni"
[4] Miklos Radnoti, "Seventh Eclogue"

v.

So many sleepwalkers leaping
into the mist of Brooklyn Bridge, Golden Gate,
so many limbs flailing in the waves.

Orpheus fumbles with his lyre.
Every night, gunshots—gangs
warring on the streets of Olympus.

Socrates on the east bank of the Volga:
Yediny, moguchy Sovetsky Soyuz! [5]
Atropos, drunk in the piazzas,
peddling cheap watches to the tourists.

Michael sweeps his bunker, irons his uniform.
Gabriel checks, rechecks his voicemail.
Weeks now, no word from headquarters.

vi.

Jerusalem. Gaza. Tibet. Sudan. Burma. Phalluses
of trade blazing beneath a satellite sky. Fumes
wafting from manholes. Tiananmen. Chernobyl.
　　Mama! I've forgotten how to sing! [6]
　　Tun Jihn Yu

Ah, Brunetto, io stesso faccio fatica a riconoscermi.
Ciacco, non piangere per la patria.
Tutto il mondo è diventato il Getsemani!

Forgive me for eating this bountiful meal.
Forgive me for sleeping beneath this roof.
Forgive me for making love to my wife.
Forgive me for everything I fail to see and do
and avenge. Forgive me for this insular life.

---

[5] from the National Anthem of the Soviet Union
[6] Vladimir Mayakovsky, "A Cloud in Trousers"

vii.

The indicator and indicated:
seppuku on the steps of the temple,
fading together in a pool of nonsense.

protean atomic strands shifting
a priori a posteriori fracturing & centripetal

The hypotenuse is a broken arm.
The compass is a roulette wheel.

$abcdfgik2x2=6$
incarnation absolute chromosomal & karmic
$f(x)$ amidst entropy must in turn beget

The shortest distance
between two points is numbness.

viii.

Brain of man, hemorrhaging, bereft
of divinity, cries out, groping for its raft
of reason: then fuzz, descent, oblivion.

Heart of nature, trapped in a ruptured hull,
forsaken angel flagging in a sea of indifference,
foundered in the barbarian darkness.

Macro to micro, frantic clusters, molecules
huddling like shivering prisoners: ultimate
nucleation, chemistry reduced to a mob hug,
a final flood of stone: *ubiquitous sepulchrum.*

ix.

The end of time
is the beginning of time,
and time itself is timeless.

The dreamer is born.
And with the dreamer,
a dream that begins and ends.

The dream subsumes the dreamer,
and the dreamer the dream,
collapsing into timelessness.

Timelessness too is a dream.
The dream ends and thus the dreamer.
What remains is neither time nor timelessness.
What remains is neither dream nor dreamer.
What remains can neither begin nor end.

x.

Possibility
is spawned by impossibility, sentience born of insentience.
In an un-beginning, void:

Then something from un-something
emerges, life sired by lifelessness—accidental, immaculate,
effect devoid of cause itself becoming cause:

Space incarnate hoists its crusted lid,
blinks, recalls its own unutterable name: Adam wakes on cue,
stretches in the protean dawn. Eve waits in the wings.

The dream resumes.

xi.

Weeds sprout, coyotes
sniff the warming air;
roaches twitch their antennae.

A chemical sky clears;
the fugitive sun returns.
Judas's coins are placed
over the eyes of the dead.

The rolling wagon is stopped.[7]
When the full moon arrives,

---

[7] *I Ching,* Section 44 (Kou)

a breeze blows over the water.[8]
Jen Kuan Wei Chi

The nest is rebuilt.
The cattle are found.[9]
The plums ripen and fall.

Above us, marbles forever circling marbles,
flickers of light in the untraceable beyond.

xii.

Juliet cooks as I watch the game.
A five o'clock squall soaks the new flowerbed.
In the evening, we sit outside, counting fireflies,
planning conquests as things bloom and molder.

Next week Achilles, my old college pal, will visit.
Next spring I'll pay off our mortgage.
Autumns come and go, each more exquisite than the last.
I wrinkle, my bones grow brittle, the shadow converges.

Afterwards, I hover for a moment, desires flurrying:
so much loved, so much left undone. As my memory
departs—a healed pigeon again taking flight—
I'm cleansed in preparation for the next go-around.

Indeed, all is one—divine, absurd, conflicted.

---

[8] *I Ching,* Section 48 (Jing)
[9] *I Ching,* Section 32 (Heng)

The First Story
Lana Hechtman Ayers

> *What would happen if one woman told the truth about her life?*
> *The world would split open.*
>
> —Muriel Rukeyser

The first story is not about light or apples.
The first story is about the woods,
the woman in the red hood, the wolf.

About the path siren flowers call you off of.
About leaving a trail only crows can follow.

The first story is about a witch, a bright house
made of gingerbread, which is to say, gluttony.
There are cinders in the hearth that sift to nothing.

Imagine hair long enough to climb, a mother's lies.
All stories are about innocence. All stories are about loss.

But the first story is about the glossy dark,
about what happens when
you close your eyes.

There is a fire in the woods.
Only Baba Yaga has the magic to call it forth.

Follow a trail of shattered bones
and scattered stones and you will find
her blind chicken-legged house.

Sift every poppy seed with your tongue by morning
and her magic will appear to become yours.

Beware appearances.
Once you have sown fire
every story is about burning down.

But before this, the first story is about the dark.
Hark—the wolf inhabits the dark.

When you close your eyes, he is there,
a river of teeth and claws.
He will tear you apart if you do not stop him.

Do not stop him.
How else to transform?

The first story is not about creation.
The first story is about the thatched dark.
Do not be so eager to light the match.

If you are cold, hold yourself close.
If you are hungry, eat desire.

If you are terrified, sing the fear to sleep.
The first story is about the big silence,
dark before illuminating words were spoken.

This is the first story,
This is our story—close your eyes, listen.

How the Aztecs Conquered Cortés
Elizabeth Barrette

He crossed the ocean
to become a *conquistador*
and make his mark on the New World.

There he made allies
and enemies,
set the tribes against each other,
and declared himself victorious.

But the Aztecs were nothing
if not masters of death and black magic,
and so they summoned a *civatateo*.
She appeared at the crossroads
with her hands and face
painted white with *ticitl* chalk
and crossbones on her ragged dress.

The dying priests gave her a charm
to make her seem human again
and told her where to find him.
Laughing, she kissed their pocked faces
and bid them give her regards to
Tezcatlipoca and Tlazolteotl.

Then the *civatateo* put on the face
that the world would come to know
as Doña Marina, and with that
she seduced Cortés.

For years she fed on him, slowly,
gorging herself on his greed and ambition.
In time she disgorged a son to him,
made in his image,
blood and spit and sweat.
She sucked the strength out of him
and replaced it with lingering weakness,
then sent him home to his precious Spain
to spread it.

Even as it grew,
the Spanish empire engulfed
the seeds of its own destruction.

Cortés complained to the crown
that he had financed the expeditions
with his own funds, and was now
heavily in debt. The crown
declined his claim on the royal treasury,
busy with its own concerns.

He slunk back to Seville,
sullen and bitter.
Doña Marina tasted him then
and knew she had waited long enough.
This time, when she bit him,
she drank her fill.

Dysentery, the doctors called it,
or perhaps pleurisy—
never knowing that the *conquistador*
had been conquered at last by the Aztecs.

At the funeral,
Doña Marina painted her face with grief
and warned her son
not to smile so sharply.

The Magician's Assistant
Penny-Anne Beaudoin

Tonight I'm going to disappear.

I disappear every night, I know, but tonight I'm not coming back.

He will look for me but never find me, that withered wizard. This
sorcerer's apprentice has been watching and learning for years, and now I
know all the tricks of his trade, and a few more besides.

Yes, and I know my little master for what he is too—
        more sham than shaman
        conjuring more doo-doo than voodoo.

I'm his 'Ta-Da' girl.
   I never speak.
   Seen but not heard, that's me.
A showgirl smile in stiletto heels, it's my job to
     smile and point to the hat
     smile and step from the magic closet
     smile and bow to the audience.

Sometimes though, my carefully painted lips want to pull themselves
back over my perfect pearly whites in a wolfish snarl, and I have to pinch
my tongue between my incisors to keep from snapping at the air.

Smiling has become such a brutal discipline.

He doesn't seem to notice.

I'm not surprised.

His prestidigitation takes all his concentration these days.

     Prestidigitation.
        From the Latin *praesto digiti*—
        performing fingers.
  The hand is quicker than the eye
     or at least it used to be.

These days there's nothing up his sleeve. The fingers that used to
transport me to magical realms

(and not just on stage either)
have stumbled and slowed
fumbled and forgotten.

And over the years
the more they've sputtered
the more my costume has shrunk
until now it's little more than a couple of sequins in the front
a shiny strand of sateen up the back
—all part of redirecting the audience's attention, as he so patiently
explained to me.
So every night I prance in front of his adoring public
nearly naked but smiling radiantly
giving them all something nice to look at
while he tries to focus on his bogus hocus-pocus.

Hocus-pocus.
From the Latin, *hoc est corpus meum*—
this is my body.
And oh! the things he's done to my body!
Cramming my ears with gold coins
stuffing my mouth with endless strings of hankies.
I've been blindfolded
bound
levitated
disappeared and
(his personal favourite)
sawed in half.
He *loves* doing that.

Driving the rigid blade in rhythmic thrusts
deeper and deeper into my soft centre
grinning at me the way he does when we're in bed
and he's splitting me in two the other way.
("*C'mon, baby, smile!*")
But on stage he gets to divide and conquer
while everyone watches
("*Smile, baby, smile!*")
and Abracadabra!
doesn't *that* just make the old magic wand snap to attention!

I always smile when he tells me to
        knowing how to fake it onstage and off...

I wonder if he remembers that circus matinee we did years ago.

He was about to pull a rabbit out of his hat
        and the poor creature must have been sick or something
        or maybe Fartus Magnus just waited too long

but he reached in and yanked out this
        glassy-eyed cadaver
        spittle glistening around its cleft lip
        flaccid body hanging long, limp and loose in his feeble grasp.

        ("Mommy, what's wrong with Mister Bunny?")

In a macabre attempt to cover up the obvious
he shook the furry carcass at the audience
in imaginary animation.

But it was too late.
        He knew it was dead.
                I knew it was dead.
And the audience
        gagging on their popcorn
        and choking on their cotton candy
        certainly knew it was dead.

With a heart-sickening thump, he dropped the remains back in the
hat and threw it at me. I caught it with one hand and carried it out of
the glare of the spotlight, tucking it away behind the magic table before
returning to the centre ring.

        And I never once stopped smiling.

He blamed me of course, and during the next trick left me sweltering
in the magic closet, reappearing me an instant before I too succumbed.

        ("Smile, bitch, SMILE!")

I got the message though, and from then on made sure the rabbit
was healthy, or at least in the land of the living before every show.

But now I'm sick of him and his dumbo mumbo-jumbo
　　with its impotent illusions and passionless pretence.
I'm on the hunt for some sexy sorcery
　　　a salty wet witchery
　　　　　a delightfully delicious devilry
　　　　　　　a warm moist magic.
It must be out there somewhere.　There must be someplace where a
woman
　　　　doesn't have to smile as she's being sliced in two
　　　　where she can speak out loud an incantation of her own
　　　　where she can indulge her appetite for the metaphysical
　　　　　and the physical.
　　　　　　　Especially the physical.

　　And if no such place exists
　　　I'm powerful enough now to conjure one up.

　　So tonight I'm going to teach an old dog a new trick.

　　　Tonight I'm going to disappear.

　　　　(And I'm taking the rabbit with me!)

The Witch's Burning
Emma Bolden

Each flick of his tongue against my foot
　　　　a smoothness I didn't expect
　　　　　　　fire so sudden logs high stacked by lovers
　　　　how bright the first tongue
licked malleolus traced tibia knee
　　　I could not look at the sky
　　　　　　　all was a gray through eyes blanked
　　　as smoke stroked
his lips in the dark dog-warm against
　　　　the flat of my foot
　　　　　　　became pain became not became flame
　　　　melting to inside of thigh
his teeth pierced to possess and I
　　　gave over possession gave up body
　　　　　　　gone of flesh the color flashed upwards

of its own accord until I
of him had tasted my mouth an open
            gulped smoke as sweet water
                        my ears remembered the river hymn singing
            O glory the sweet sharp
taste of feast   seared meat on his tongue
            holding deep the history
                        of char a new self the old unfleshed
            of flesh
flayed thighs O   I took him   inside
            implored O
                        God on the cross that thief who You
            saved my breath
my breath was his breath and each breath
            a gift given taken each
                        smooth flicker licked the lids off my eyes
            under sky's blue skin
stretched by the river frozen to mirror
            the syrup sharp stench
                        of foot unfooting itself
            black blossoms
the char taste of feast when I licked he
            rose high
                        as my chin the fire stroked sure as a skill
            as a hand
stroked and softly we were our own
            melting
                        fire a stillness I watched and the sun
            in its separate burning
the ice threw off its blanket below
            the hinge of my knee
                        bent the memory kneeling
            down to him
his teeth a secret I held
            in the town square
                        shadows cast flame like flame
            wild
my breasts bit bleeding I held his child
            hidden
                        child daughter a wail inside my wail
            behind the peel
beneath my flesh a hope opened
            of mine own

                         peeling thigh to not thigh not foot
            he held in his right
hand slipped itself through my skirts
            to find
                         not knotted rope not run not body no
            the small
pink bundled beneath
            red inside
                         not mouth not wanted not water
            not again giving
not any more mirror the rivers of water
            not again giving up
                         throat dissolve resolve terminus wanted
            giving up
became not snow the waters he washed
            calendula candlewax
                         child daughter wail hymn my disappear
            hope of water
to vanish my scent off his body
            his hand held
                         the twig its starting flame

Sweet Tooth
Robert Borski

He could not remember
the last time

he had been to an actual
dentist

(the old country, perhaps?),
although he

did have a dim recollection
of a late

night encounter with an oral
hygienist once

where the two, pre-necking,
had a

major row about plaque
vs. platelets,

but when his throbbing tooth
kept him

awake well into sunrise, he
knew he

could avoid the inevitable
no longer.

Dread was not something that
had ruled

his unlife beyond the brightening
sky or

sharp splinters of wood, so
when he

heard the dentist's strict injunction
against sweets,

"You would be well advised, sir,
to avoid

anything but the occasional
dessert,"

it was not without a certain
degree of regret.

Still, the next night, equipped
with a gold

incisor (no toxic silver for him,
thank you),

he began his new regimen—
not a one

of the vessels he supped from
having the

lingering claret-like sweetness
he had so

come to love. After a century
of indulgence,

diabetics, like ice cream melting
in the sun,

had become just another fondess
he would

have to do without; while deep down
in his

cabinet of dirt, no matter how much
he licked

the remnants of caked blood on
his lips,

it would seldom again taste enough
of frosting.

Thirteen Ways of Looking at a Vulture
Bruce Boston

after Wallace Stevens

I
The vulture is a dark songbird.
Its raucous cries herald
The disemboweling of the dead.

II
I was of a single mind,
Like a colony of vultures circling
A lone man in the desert.

III

The vulture volplaned on the heated air,
Lord of sky and earth below.

IV

A man and a woman
Are one.
A man and a woman and a vulture
Are a ghastly *ménage à trois*.

V

I am not sure which to favor,
The dusty music of my heart
Or the rash music of war,
The vulture's keen eye
Or nothing at all.

VI

A sandstorm turned the window
To thickly pebbled glass.
The silhouette of a vulture
Crossed it, to and fro,
The mood cast
By its broad shadow
Was tenacious.

VII

O fat men of Middleton,
Why do you conjure birds of gold?
Do you not feel the vulture
Nibbling at your toes?

VIII

I know the vulture dreams
Of being shiny as a raven,
Iridescent as a peacock,
Spotless as a swan
Upon a pellucid pond.

IX

When the vulture flew out of sight
It left behind a landscape
Stripped of carrion.

X

At the sight of vultures
Flying in formation at dusk,
Even men of certain faith
Fear the Prince of Darkness.

XI

He had entered
The glass carriage
When he was startled
By the ungainly shape
Of a vulture perched
Upon its translucent roof.

XII

Death is everywhere.
The vulture must be flying.

XIII

It was evening all day
Beneath the radiation clouds.
It was raining
And it was going to rain.
The vulture feasted
At its pleasure.

Postcards from Mars
G. Sutton Breiding

Earth you are a fading teardrop
between moon and moon,
the petrified skies I stare at like an idiot,
in dreams of grey rain
whispering around inside helmets,
like quicksand, cleavage, cruel pages,

Earth in a dewdrop, a snowflake, a cricket's eye.
Smell of dark grasses; tangerine.
Something passes through the dawn, shadowlike,
from crack to crack, under days of quartz.

Old autumn shores:
redheads in the sky. O moon and moon,
the light that rattles. What is evening, here?
Delirium of palms, linen, orange moss,
long echo of alabasterness.

Mile and miles out today:
red salt flats, black hermit pillars.
Sounds like wind through pines.
Nothing but ghosts, mica bones, mirage
of porcelain cities.

Haunting observations. The not-birds, the Earth
inside us, bitter coffee,
insect scuttle, the brushing away
of webs, hair, snowbreath,
none of it there.

Relics of lost poets.
Archives of echo, fragments of voice.
Silver lips pressed against helmets.
Poems made of sand, crystal, pubic flesh.
Infinite Mars of her mouth.

Entities hush by, sparkling wet silk.
Images of steam vents, old brick, rooftop watertowers.
Crackles of language. Caressable phrases.
A necklace of ships toward Jupiter.
We watch, frozen, clutching our vials.

Landscape of tanager, oriole, gold cicada.
Look at that city—
the Imortalists died there, ranting and drooling.
Odd sensations. Taste of salt and lemon.
Quiver of buttocks under my tongue.
Cybersirens in digital seas. Red prose,
gazelles of thought, a box of alphabets.

Smell of iron in rain but there is no RAIN.
Flash-winds, flash-memories of whiskey
and ancient orchards: smell of rotting apples
and rust under these lead pipe skies. Bunkers

of concrete, spaceship detritus. Open lines
on RadioMars.

Remains of movements in the dark, pieces
of afterimage, mirror-deliria, apparition of rivers.
Music, like if cats were glass.
The burlap curtain between dread and panic.
Patience; accidents; unknown footprints.
Our spines split double for each moon,
cold metal in our throats.

Insane robots: cliche of: reality of.
AI myth and lore. Running headfirst into walls
of cinnabar. Virulence of isolation.
Robot/flesh. Othernesses, mysterians, oids.
Braided wires hanging from sounds of powdered rust.
Robot/apocalypse. Clones teleporting
through solid space.
Cliff dwellings full of headcasings.

Sciencefiction. Freight trains.
The titanium scribe bent to its task:
glass quill, spirit lamp, radiation suits,
jetpaks, world of pure breath.
Across these endless sands.
Hangovers in orbit, hangovers on Mars.
Grind insects, hipbones, into inkpowder.
Humanfiction. Sex with ghosts and language.

Distant ululations just at about late afternoon.
Undulations under the sand, red waves
across the paper, peripherals of shadow.
Out into the Arena of Dissolve.
Underground chambers, geode eyes,
something porous in grey holes.

Drama in the Black Dome:
her hair stood 2 feet straight up.
Raving about squirrel skins, Youngstown,
parallel universes. I watched her, drinking
something gold; watched her and thought of her
in panties and hoody.

Mirages of smokestacks,
medieval angels, snow and weeds. Bridges
thrumming under clack of heels. O rain
on streets, leafless trees, metal awnings.

Dark circles opening beneath us: into
ether pools, vistas of violet photons,
photographs of exploding shuttle euphoria. Who
laments, out there, in the dusk?

Cinnamon fills the mouth.
Honeycomb minds blur together.
The sky tunes us far from you, O Earth,
on trips to suns and suns beyond our lifespans.
We are the legend of the red planet.

Discovery: narcotic lichen.
In fields of lark and phoenix. Artefact wreckage.
Catchphrases of prophecy. We chew and sit.
Blue curtains fall into pools of blue sand.
Giant sundew along the marble docks.
Tall dancers like canna flowers swaying.
Snow hissing into braziers where we warm our memories.

Tomorrow will be tomorrow.

Flotsam of empty spacesuits.

These orange beaches.

Manipulation
Shelly Bryant

Click. Off went the lamp on the lectern. His gaze rose toward the faces in
the room. He found on them not quite the incredulity he expected, but
outright disdain.

"I know," he began uncomfortably, "that it seems impossible that the
mind can be used to realign the body's molecules, but it is a fact. Once
one has ascertained the molecular structure of an object, he or she can
align the body's cells to pass right through it. It's all a matter of making
sure the cells don't collide in the process."

"Do you claim to have achieved the ability to do so?"

"Yes, I do."

Snorts of laughter greeted the assertion.

"I'm not the first, of course," he added. "It was done thousands of years ago, but with the opposite goal in mind. Water's molecular structure is so loosely organized that the human body normally passes through it. Long ago, one wise man and his protégé managed to rearrange their molecular structure, aligning it with that of the water so that they would not sink in it. Those who witnessed it credited it to supernatural powers. But it was not miraculous at all, just a mental manipulation of molecules."

As he finished his spiel, he dabbed at the perspiration breaking out on his brow, seemingly incongruent with the frigidity of the gazes that met his eyes.

> desperation's sweat
> beading in anxiety
> faces icy stares

"Show us." The challenge, rising above the snickers that filled the room, was issued more with derision than a desire for evidence, but he was prepared all the same.

He picked up his lecture notes, holding the pages up in front of him. He placed his index finger on the front page and concentrated. Slowly, before the unbelieving eyes of the audience, his finger began to protrude through the other side of the paper.

Silence.

When he extracted his finger again, he beamed at the audience. Their reaction stunned him. He had not expected to hear words such as "magic tricks," "nonsense," or "scam," but that was exactly what came to him from the muttering crowd.

He knew he couldn't afford to lose them. This was his only chance to gain respectability.

scholar's greatest fear
tarnished name forever lost
or made laughingstock

He looked desperately around the room, his eyes finally falling on his research partner. She had advised him not to go public yet, especially not in this venue where the brightest minds were gathered. But to his relief, she simply nodded, and then rose from her seat.

Silence fell once again. At least she was a well recognized figure in the field. The multitude of articles she had published in leading journals around the globe ensured that she would not be easily ignored or scorned.

She walked to the stage, as ungainly a figure as ever, but still composed and cool. She extended her hand towards him.

"Shall we?" she asked.

an overture
face-saving hand within reach
assistance offered

He hated doing this, but knew it was the only way. It required trusting her ability to align the molecules of her body as much as he trusted his own. He'd shown himself, through their months of work together, singularly unwilling to do that. He loved her mind, but somehow found her person to be less than worthy of his trust.

He smiled weakly and lifted his hand toward hers. Their palms seemed to merge into one. This time, he heard from the audience the gasps he had hoped to hear, rather than the guffaws that bombarded him earlier.

He held his breath as their hands seemed to fuse into a single, shared organ. He swelled with pride as murmurs of amazement arose from those looking on. He raised his eyes toward hers, and what he saw there chilled him. Shrinking back, he failed to extract his hand from hers.

inseparable
molecular alignment
manipulated

Custody
Rosalind Casey

Dear Diary

I saw Mom crying again
Even though the fighting stopped
Even though she says Don't worry sweetie
Cause you'll be back before you know it
But her lips go tight when she says it
Like a bean pod
Dead before it's ripe.

I don't want to go away
It's cold where Uncle Hades lives
Too cold for flowers
Too cold for my friends to come
There's no one talking but the gardener
And he has hard and shiny diamond eyes
And a skin crawl smile.

He can't be a real gardener if he doesn't grow flowers.

But I'll go I guess
I'm tired of the fighting
Of all the sharp edged words that
Taste wrong in my mouth
Words like compromise and
Implied contract
Words like single parent household
That make Mom's eyes go snap
Like catclaw in the bracken.

They always talk so much
And Uncle Zeus uses such a reasonable tone
It just makes mom madder til she says
You filthy hypocrite—
And Sephi, honey, go and play outside—
But Uncle Hades doesn't talk at all
He just stares and smiles and scowls.
Sometimes he stares at me.

But I'll go I guess
Cause it can't be all that bad
Uncle Hades sometimes whispers in a
dry dirt voice
That he'll make me queen.
The library has storybooks
where queens are always beautiful
with flowers in their hair.

Besides, it's not forever
like they said maybe
it's only a few months
And I tell Mom that I'll be back and
everything will be the same
And she looks up and says Will it, Baby?
Will you be my little girl?
And I say yes,
I'll always be your Flower Maiden
But then her face goes dead
Like winter.

Other Difficulties
C. S. E. Cooney and Nicole Kornher-Stace

PART I: THE FAMILIAR

Dear Fetch,

Since our witch died, I've been lone-wolfing it
Shore-padding, wood-prowling, you know the way
Hey—for three wild weeks, even did the Sister Cities:
Queen's Keep and Leech
Wow. What a howl.

A lousy and particular itch, how I miss her
Often have to shake this skin
Walk as man among men (don't laugh)
You were right, Fetch
Each passerby turned back, glanced twice:
"Don't I know you?" in their shaky, shattered voices
"Almost sure I know you..."

"Naw, sir, ma'am—nope we never met
Least, not direct—though, in point of fact
T'was mayhap my grin lured your girl off-path
The dusty track, the known map—and was she dressed in scarlet?
Cheeks like apples? Leaf-lips sugary as maples?
Why—I let her mount my hoary back, the wee red rocking cradle
Riding, rocking, riding me that hard white road
To witch's hut, my hearth and home
Where we laid her bare:
Heart for cauldron, teeth for curtains, a thigh for you to gnaw on, Fetch
Her goldilocks to hang from chandelier of braided hair."

(I wonder, is that fixture still there?)

Mostly strangers mosey by, worm-eyed, queasy
But come the grieving ones to hang upon my sleeve
Inspect my shade and shape, caress my shifty contours,
sob rapturous:
"My drowned! My crushed! My long-lost! My storm-tossed!
Beloved, clambered up from slumber and the very depths!"

It pleases me to fondle the bereaved
Squeeze and tickle, pinch and prick at, trick and tease them
Ease this itch, this emptiness, do some mischief—a memorial
To one whose middle name was cruelty
At dawn confess, to tears of bliss like pearls on the pillow:

"I am not your lover, ghoul-crawled from the grave
Nor husband strayed, nor father, brother, son
Merely, a Familiar who mislaid his family, went walking
The witch's wayward pet now gone a little wild."

Fetch, what next? Where to? And how?
I don't remember life before our witch
Her roof of thatch, her candy glass
Am I wolf by birth? Or worse? Torqued up from baby bones
Or golemed from the garden earth, her fevered spit
Her breath that smelled of primrose?

I was her own dark mirror, ranked higher than the bell and candle
Crucial as the grimoire that she shelved next to her cookbooks
Right beside the cage you crouched in, dearest Fetch
Singing seven harmonies in no known key

All those days we lived together and for her, I was happy
Now I'm free.

But enough about me—
How are you faring?

Your devoted,

Catch

PART 2: THE FETCH

Dearest creature,

How clearly I remember her last days—
hawking and wheezing in that sluttish bed,
the thick black blood on heaps of tatted handkerchiefs,
each with its thread-snagged violets, each with its corpse's
monogram, its sweet sweet stain
of tears. (I too recall the chandelier. How not? It swings
its pendulum above my head at night, back and forth,
or circling, when no wind stirs the trees.) I mopped
her sweating brow, I caught her witch-puke
in a vase; eleven eager fingers tallied out the rasps
till she was gone. How odd
to watch one's own long face go still! It brings to mind
the people's gravestones with their pretentious wings
and their Not Dead Only Sleepings, their Not Lost
But Gone Befores—although eventually there was
a certain smell. I had to toss her in the soup.

(You'd scratched the door and whined, too stirred
to slip that sodden skin, to sprout some bloody *thumbs*. I turned
the knob for you—smoothed with the sweaty palms
of sacrifices rattling the lock—ah, what we do, my friend,
in the pursuit of Science!—and off you went. The door
snicked shut; the rattle sounded in her skinny ribs
like baskets tumbled down a stair. A melancholy glee.
And here we are.)

Ah, love, why don't you pay a visit? This place is
as empty as a staged death's grave, as cold

98

as wish denied. I don't light fires much. What need
have I of heat? But I remember fondly
casting shadow-puppets, you and I and our
nineteen combined fingers, while she lay snoring
in her pilfered silks. The country people bring me things,
as well—fear-gifts, blood-gifts, fripperies—first-fruits,
a bleeding honeycomb, a foetal lamb to flay for gloves.
Surplus daughters. Eggs. Loaves. Brooding widowers.
(These latter often bring themselves.) They take
my door for hers, my face for hers, my thighs.
And I take all the rest.

May the wilds keep you well. My door is *mine*—
and yours, if you so choose. Until that time I'll watch
for you, I'll ravel out the shadows of the hills and trees
to parse your scraggled shape. I won't lie: it's lonely here. Her ghost
scrapes at the pane. And in the glass, is it my face
peering back at me? Or hers, barred outside, staring in?

An erstwhile

Fetch

Prince
Bryan D. Dietrich

*If Mother could only see me now...as a very feminine woman...a nurse no
less, in a world full of men...*
—Princess Diana, in Sensation Comics #1

I.

We all leave Paradise. I left my prints
there, on everything, when I was young.
Each orchid, every smooth grove of olive, tongue
of turk's cap, on silverswords, archer fish, hyacinths,

on even the tarsiers and turtles, as if my hands
had to know the shapes of all I would soon be
letting go. The trade I made was no Thermopylae,
no Miletus, but my mother's promise, these bands

I wear, bound me to more than just my sisters,
their island, their Amazon days, my own lonely nights....
So when, near the end of Paradise, down by its bights,
that man washed ashore, a man as lost to the bluster

of disaster as we had once been; when, still waterlogged with war
he saw me, said, *Woman*.... Why wonder that I brought him to my door?

II.

He saw me, said woman, as wonder, what brought
him to my door. Both urge and end, his own long fall.
But I was no soldier, not then. The din and drawl
of war remained as abstract as his fever-fraught

dreams. Oh, and what fine fancy I must have starred
in! Though I spent days tending my flyboy's wounds,
though he understood, intimately, the sound
of my voice, the fact of my hand as it carried

his own to my breast before he died, even then,
with memories of his mission, his crash, returning,
with all the inconvenient evidence of my being
real, still he wanted me as Valkyrie, as sin.

Me, from a land where he was just in jest.
He, from a land where I could only arrest.

III.

He, from a land where I would only arrest,
where kiss and fist were lovers that caressed,
where men were women's last excuse for less....
History-, mystery-, breast-, vagina-less....

It's a wonder we could communicate at all.
Even when I brought him back, used our science—a small
matter, but as far from his own as cathode from caul—
even after I'd dragged him back from death's mead hall,

even then, he imagined me imagined manna,
saw me as a proof of God, perhaps Valhalla.

But then I guess *he*.... He was what? Shangri-La
to me? Abomination? Something new. Our law

said he could not stay, but also not to kill.
They'd need a hero to bring him back. They need one still.

IV.

They needed a hera to bring him back. Need?
One still wonders if indeed they needed *me*.
Then. The distance from that world to this, agreed,
was not so fraught with fright as mine to his, but he

was still with me then. I counted myself
lucky to have a steady job. Though keeping him
out of trouble left me breathless, it's not as if
there were a dearth of dastardly to help keep trim.

No, I don't know that—on coming to your shores,
on finally finding a place for the plane, the rest
all which vanishes desires—that the mores
of this land struck me as particularly less,

or how you herded unheard women was, well, surprise.
All I knew was what I gained, a ewe lost in eyes.

V.

All I knew was what I gained, a ewe lost in eyes.
Here, they were ubiquitous: catcalls, gawks, cocks,
assward assumptions. After one has fought for the prize,
beaten better sisters to blood and sand, one balks

when, even *after* the arena, the audience remains.
Back in Paradise, I had to earn the *right* to be banished,
had to win the Games, master chains, take the reins
of my kanga mount and—so tasked, masked, I vanished—

prove myself to my mother, placate the Queen,
salve the substance of my dream. Saving even one man....
It seemed, in the end, such a small endeavor,
returning him to what he was: Capt. Steve Trevor.

But leaving didn't relieve me my star status. It stuck,
the liberty of the lamb. I never learned to pass the buck.

VI.

Libertine or lamb, I never learned to pass the buck.
But *had* I passed him; had I left him to another,
to my sisters to save, let him die, invited a quick fuck
and even quicker forgetting; had I made him brother,

friend, astonishing but temporary, acquaintance
only; had I left this world of yours to its own
devices, all that power piled up (no maintenance)
between your legs; had I eschewed the throne

of this Regent, that Reich; had I abhorred your war
altogether, left you, left him, to fend for yourselves;
had I abandoned you all to sea, to mountain, at my door,
all I ever learned from dodging bullets—shells,

lead—would've been to not end dead. Instead, my blunder?,
I shared with him my shackles. Is it any wonder?

VII.

Woman I shared with him. But my shackles?
I wonder. Perhaps that's what I've left on the altar
for all of you. By being this being that's lack-less,
eternal, Hercules strapped in a backless halter,

by sharing my shoulders, my ripples, my pecs,
my faith in the failure of some guy with specs,
by fighting, as praxis, your axis, your evil,
becoming your Eve and survival, your rival,

by leaving my land for apotheosis,
by being both symptom and prognosis,
well.... Bombshell or no, I've left you ticking.
I've left you what's left after apple picking.

I've left you it all. Pain. Common sense.
What we all must leave. Paradise, I left my prince.

In the Astronaut Asylum
Kendall Evans and Samantha Henderson

> *"I gave my life to guesswork*
> *on the ambiguous hope*
> *the stars could be real"*
> > From "Asylum for Astronauts"
> > By Bruce Boston & Marge Simon

I. The Saturday Night Dance

Come all ye to Bedlam Town
When sun come up the stars go down
When stars go down beneath our feet
Then 'tis a merry time to meet

In the Astronaut Asylum
Events sometimes transpire
As if on the second planet out
From Aldebaran

Ex-Astronauts are madmen
They dream of decaying orbits
And the passionate embrace
Of isomorphic aliens

The doors of the asylum
Are like airlock doors
Aboard a starship
Or perhaps like wheeled hatches
Between pressurized chambers
In a submarine

In the Astronaut Asylum
Even the doctors and the staff
Often believe they are on Mars
Inhabiting sheltered underground corridors
And cabins
Or strapped in shipboard limbo
Somewhere between the stars

The central dome is pressurized
With an exotic atmosphere
The star-farer who resides therein
The only one who might survive inside—
I know
Because the other patients
Told me so

III. Theories of Madness

Come, let's go to Bedlam Street
Star-faring ladies for to meet
Who stare transfixed upon the glow
Of Earthly seas above, below

During Thursday's group therapy session
One of the west-wing Astronauts
Advances her innovative theory:

Here is the secret (don't flinch
While I whisper in your ear; you know,
Despite that pinched lip, that glazed look
You carefully cultivate, pretending that
None of this has any,
Anything to do with you), here 'tis—
All go mad, not just the far-travelers,
Not just those surfers of light-speed,
Not merely those who've dared the wormholes,
No—
All.

Somewhere out past the orbit of the moon
Madness comes—
Slow, mind, for those who think they travel safe,
Travel sane and measured—
Sometimes they die before the disease rooted deep
Within them hatches,
Like an alien egg
Unleashing what into our minds?
What fungus grows about our eyes
Before we succumb?
Live long enough, and it comes to this.

The Cosmonauts in the East Wing
Offer contradictory explanations
Maintaining the human body
Is like a SETI antenna
Receiving messages
From diverse alien civilizations
Strewn throughout our Milky Way
Galaxy, and beyond

They fashion crinkled aluminum foil helmets
To ward off the signals
Shielding themselves
From interstellar insanity
And the maddening music
Of the spheres

IV. A Conversation
With Your Uncle-Astronaut

On Bedlam Row, in madman's mire
We orbit swift, a dizzy gyre
Or bask in dying stars' dim glow
And dream of things you'll never know

Or maybe you are the Astronaut-Uncle,
Visiting on the landscaped grounds
At a picnic table
In sunlight
Out past the triple dome shadows
During a moment so real
(despite taking place within
Asylum gates)
You perceive each leaf of grass,
Every blade-shadow

As one of you turns toward the other
And says: "Listen—
After the last Apollo Mission
I felt concerned
Mankind had forgotten how to walk
Upon the Moon—"

One of you pauses,
Contemplative of a cloud
And the unseen daylit stars beyond.
"Now, after being stranded on Ceres,
After penetrating the surfaces
Of Jovian moons
And dancing upon Asylum ceilings,
I feel confident
One might step anywhere."

V. The Youngest Cosmonaut

Come with me to Bedlam Row
And see the mad go to and fro
These Astronauts who only trust
Their phantom bags of lunar dust

One of the cosmonauts
Is only 6 years old
On the cusp
Of becoming five
Suffering from reverse entropy
Ever since his final re-entry

This is either gospel truth
Or perhaps the staff
Has confused him
With someone else

One of the orderlies
Recently lamented:
"Communication is impossible
We record his words
& Run the tapes backwards

"But no one can recall:
Precisely what was it he said
In his reverse Russian
When he last spoke to us
Tomorrow?"

VI. Epilog

Three Cosmonauts
Inexplicably disappeared
During the recent solar eclipse
& No one could explain
The staff's panic attacks

Slip Bedlam's locks,
Hide Bedlam's Keys;
We'll drown beneath
These star-filled seas

On nights when the moon is full
The Astronauts stride
Thru sparkling lunar dust
Traipsing asylum corridor floors all aglow
Leaving luminous footprints to follow

Corrected Maps of Your City
Kendall Evans and David C. Kopaska-Merkel

Every convenience store has them:
So shiny and bright,
Each street name legible,
They fold and refold perfectly
(Your first clue they are alien technology)

Behind your building, no-name alley,
You know, the one with
Piles of garbage instead of trash cans
The map calls it "shortcut alley"
You've never been down it
But today you think "why not?"

It shortcuts to a place quite Escher-ish
A place with arching side-up down staircases
Where climbing figures contradict
Gravity's orientations—
A place that cannot be real

Beneath a street-lamp,
In sodium-colored light
He reads the map-legend's fine print
"This map is self-correcting
Analogous to reality itself"
How could that be?

The street lengthens as he walks
The panorama shifts
The sushi shop occupies both sides
Of the street simultaneously
For seven blocks.
(Another clue;
The city itself, he decides,
Must be constructed with alien technology)

He is hungry,
Stops at one of the bright efficient counters
Where a petite Asian girl takes his order
The cook, behind a bamboo screen,
Seems...large,
And maybe he possesses
Quivering antennae
The zebra fish sashimi has hooves
But no internal organs
The rice is purple
Tastes like beef...
It's delicious

That's enough adventure
For one day, I decide—
But retracing my steps
I find endless vistas
Sidestreets
Shimmering curtains of
Polychromatic light
Crowds that seem increasingly
Diverse,
But what I do not find
Is Broad St., my home address
No longer on the map
Somehow shifted off the charts
Of probability

At this precise point
My Corrected Map of the City
Said to me:
"I have scanned the schizmatic breakthrus
The fractured road warrior antics
The false turnings, the inspired route deviations
And now, finally,
I am ready to accompany you
To the highest ground, the intricate afterspaces
And beyond."

The Little Sea Maid
Kendall Evans and Stephen M. Wilson

"Pride must suffer pain"

Swastika of starfish embrace
perfect pearl mollusk
heart—a strata
   of air
   to water
   to stone

Her siren song beckons
no *spiritus mecurialis*

This is the crab's garden
The glowing lake of lava
At the bottom of the sea
A congregation of diseased eels
And broken daydreams
Inhabit the mermaiden's
   caverned heart
as she remembers

   the pain
      of severed
      tongue
      and tail
   the prick
      of needles
      and knives

in too soon lost
    young dreams
unfulfilled
   (this encompassed/
expressed
    in unremitting scream)
  the pang
   of her sisters'
   sacrificial
   despoliation
But most of all the
  rejection
  (absent kiss
    of love/life)

Now
what were once
legs and even
longer ago
   a Princess's tail
have transformed—
e a c h

t e n t a c l e

```
s   8   r   &   t   a   t       p
p       i           h   i   o       u
r   o   s   j   e   r           l
  o   y   e   e               w   l
u   s       t   d   &   r
t   t   t   s   a       a       h
i   e   h   a   u   t   p   i
n   r   r   m,      g   h           m
g   s   o           h   e   a
    c   u   i   t           r       b
f   a   g   g   e   e   o  THE    a
r   r   h   n   r   y   u           c
o   s.      o   s   e   n  PRINCE k
m       f   r               d
    T   l       i   o   o               i
t   h   o       n   f       f   a       n
h   e   t       g               n       t
e   y   s           t   G   d       o
        a           h   o
    m           e   d       t
                            h
                          e d
                            e
                            p
                            t
                            h
                            s
```

111

The Drowned Town
Gemma Files

What Dahut knows (now):

How the sea makes a bad husband
but the Devil a worse lover.
The perfidy of fathers
and the mercilessness of saints.
Just how far down a fall
from a horse's back may take you.

This is wisdom,
cold and deep—
the longest embrace,
crushing air from lungs,
light from air.
Narcotic rapture, hard truth,
pulls her into darkness
where night's vast trench engulfs her.
And at the very bottom

Her mother's smokeless flame
lights up the drowned town's windows
while her coils fill up its floors;
its scaly towers, coral-grown,
like thorns,
provide her only crown.
She receives no visitors—
sends out the occasional
chandelier of memory,
brief gelid visions of
her topside self, set like lures
to drift between currents.

How Dahut looks (now):

Nothing like them, anymore;
nothing like you.
All pearl skin
and flat shark's eyes—
hair like kelp, trailing miles long,
pod-studded.

Her fin-feet flutter
as she hovers above the murk,
singing.

The tide steals her voice,
translates it to
wrack and loss, white noise, rock-riven.
An ell on every side,
whales and skates cringe from it—
rays flee, flapping like sails.
Eels and sea-snakes knot so tight
they strangle each other.

But her song is not meant for them, anyhow.

Where Dahut lives (now):

Deep, and deeper.
Neck-high in the silt
of centuries.
She can still be sought
by those who brave the gulfs,
but only at a cost.

Above, a bathysphere descends
over the shelf-lip,
an iron moon setting.
Below, she waits.
In Dahut's sunken city,
the drowned town, Ys,
the slimy streets are paved
with shell and longing.
The sea her husband
makes a jealous (if a careless)
spouse—

and a red-armored
skeleton horse roams
the caverns nearby,
its rider carrying
a prehistoric fish
perched on one wrist

like a hooded hawk,
with his helmet rusted shut.

Snow, Blood, Night
Joshua Gage

I. Mother

Winter is a time of waiting
when the world is eaten by cold and hunger
haunts the shadows. Everything is scraps
and savings, and memories hold until
the sun blesses the trees with leaves.
Where there is snow, bellies shrink
with longing, and the food is all salt
and dryness. Even apples cease
their sweetness after a time.

In the castle's cold, I wanted to feel
filled. I would haunt my mirror, naked
and run my hands across myself,
the edges of my ribs, the well
of skin that ached beneath them.
I would rock the dream of a child to sleep
all the while weeping. I sang
lullabies to our reflection,
told stories to the darkness. My daughter
must be beautiful by now,
but I have lost time to this tower.
The stumps that once were nails won't claw
the stone. Even the blood has stopped.
I cannot keep the days, cannot
tell sun from moon, cannot feel
anything but the worm of hunger
gnawing its way out of me.

II. Stepmother

Every night, I would soak
myself in the lake of the mirror
and rise, clean, a maiden untorn,
until she grew, a calf

ready for veal. Then
I could only draw scars
and wrinkles from the water.

The huntsman brought her lungs
and liver for my table,
but the mirror still spoke of winter
despite the blossoms perfuming
the trees. I will lace ribbons
to string her breath from her lungs,
carve a bone with poison
for her hair. She damns
my face with second best,
so I will bless her lips
with this apple, watch her
fall with the first red bite.

III. Daughter

Winter is a shroud the world wears
when it grows weary of the sun, and days
forget themselves to darkness. I had lived
in the woods so long, I could have been the earth
itself, dark with years of leaves and rot.
The men returned to me each night to mine
between my legs. Their stench would soak my sheets
and cling to my skin, but I didn't mind.
Night after night, they came to me, like monks
drawn to prayer. They became the bells
of my cathedral, my Book of Hours. They left
me trinkets for my flesh, gold and diamonds,
until it seemed like I was a jewel myself.

I grew numb to cold and would lie in the snow
beneath the moon. I watched the storm pull down
the stars and cling to me. Lying still,
I was just another tree or stone in the landscape,
motionless, glittering with ice as though entombed
in glass. The lord of the land discovered me
asleep, lifted me upon his horse,
and rode me to his castle. His wife is a witch
who watches me like a raven on a corpse.
But the men who love me know the secrets of iron,

the ways of lock and key. They visit me
when the moon is in a womb of clouds, and stoke
their fires. I will become the queen, bejeweled
and admired. The lady of the land withers.
Her skin is lined with years. Soon she will slip
these shoes upon her feet and learn to dance.

The Meek Shall Inherit…
(The Earthworm Speaks)
Delbert R. Gardner

Instead of being a pair of ragged claws
Scuttling across the floor of sunless ocean,
I'd rather follow my own annelid laws
And eat and undulate for locomotion.
I work in mysterious ways
My earth-moving duties to perform. A maze
Of worm-encalcined tunnels fills the earth:
We're everywhere, except in rock or sand—
A hundred thousand of us per acre of land.

The scoffers no doubt say,
"When you see one earthworm, you've seen them all.
There's hardly room for individuality."
Ah well, what do the scoffers know? Do they
Know how we build and lime our tunnel wall?
They don't know how the dirt we masticate,
Which passes through our systems and out the ends,
Gives us both locomotion and nutrition—
To eat and run is part of our condition!

And then the way we propagate our race
Without the need for difference of sex—
But each of us is male and female worm;
Our mating wears a most Platonic face:
Laid end to end, we merely swap our sperm,
Then separate, and each of us effects
The birth of his/her passionless begot—
Ingenious arrangement, is it not?
Eliminates all sorts of lovers' fights,
Paternity suits and staying awake nights
Wondering if the spouse is false or true.

And yet there will be times when I debate
About just where the scheme of things all tends,
And wonder too about free will and fate.
I feel a little lost in all the crew
Of earthy worms around me, hardly friends,
Who will not notice when I too am part
Of this dear soil in which they have their being.
And after you've moved a pound of earth, so what?
I must have moved *almost* a pound by now—
It was my greatest purpose at the start,
But now I seem to have dropped "why" for "how."
If I could feel my job accomplished aught
Within the larger scheme of this our earth—
Our sages tell us to believe, without seeing,
That what we're doing in itself has worth
And that we shouldn't try to understand
The higher purpose of life; they say have faith
In things not felt: beyond our mazy land
Of dirt and moisture there's another kind
Of world depending on ours in many ways
Incomprehensible to earthworm mind.

        Ah well, then, let it be.
Let's do our job, and someday we may see.

Creation Myth
Robert K. Gardner

Before there was a time, a world, a stone,
A mountain, dune, a woman, man, or beast,
Before the burning sands and blessed springs,
As one, the Sun and Darkness lived alone.
There was no daylight, no ghostly moon
Above, no night to chill the bones, no dawn
To end the fasting, dusk to bring the sleep,
No noontime heat to sleep away in shade.

The Darkness looked upon this empty space
And wanted it to teem with life. She told
The Sun of her desire. But he, who feared
That one to come might climb up to them, cast
Them down, usurp their rule, refused to make

New life with her. The Darkness, not content
To rule a void, caressed the Sun and told
Him softly that she would keep all beings below
And smother those who dare approach. She lay
With him and thus the Darkness conceived the world.

She brought it forth in pain, and mountains rose
Where water from her black lips touched the land,
Plants and beasts sprang where water from her brow,
And springs and lakes gushed where milk from her breast.

She looked upon what she had made and cried
With joy the tears that mixed with soil to form
Her daughters, dark like her. And she they praised
For all they saw. They built a house for her
And called her Lumal, mother of the world.

The world knew nothing of suffering, strife,
Or hunger. Nothing killed, no weapons had
The women, claws or fangs the beasts, no spikes
Or poison the plants—for Lumal nursed them all.

The Sun, made jealous at the sight, became
Enraged and tried to destroy the world.
He sent a fire that lit the sky and burnt
The night away. He scorched the forests, plains,
And mountains, turning every place to sand
Except those on which Lumal's shadow lay.
To these oases her daughters fled.

Lumal battled the Sun until they both,
In weariness, collapsed and slept an age.
The Sun was first to wake. He saw that Lumal
Was sleeping still, and so he seized the world
From where it rested on her breast. Beside
A spring, he found some women sleeping.
In the water he cooled his hands, then pressed
His fingers into the women. He made
Them narrow, flattened their chests, and turned their soft
Faces ugly and hard. He pulled out tails
And thus the world was given its men.
He fell upon the animals and from
Their mouths and paws he pulled out claws and fangs,

And from the plants, he pulled out spikes and thorns.
Thus life was given the means to end itself.

On waking, Lumal found these women, deformed
And driven mad. They howled and fought against
Their sisters. Lumal restored the peace and tried
To make them what they once had been and failed.
But she took pity on man, making him
Appear as beautiful as she herself
In woman's eyes; and so that she might be
More closely bound to man, woman was given
By Lumal the power to create
New souls, but only from the loins of man.

The Sun witnessed his evil thwarted and
Was driven mad anew. He again stole
The world from where it lay on Lumal's breast,
But held it only till she wrested it
Away from him—and still they battle.
Their fighting is the tempest in the sky,
The shaking of the ground, and they each hold
The world but always the other takes it back.
And that is why, in light and dark, the world
Spends time awash in each; and why the blue
And white sky always fills with night again;
Why once where there was unity, there's now
The clash of wills in naked opposition.

Godfather Death
Rose Lemberg

for JoSelle Vanderhooft

1. IN A WAY OF INTRODUCTION

Autumn ceases with a hiss
December lies down
and spreads her snow.
I have no emptiness
            where I can burrow in my hurt,
no hands to hold me

except my own
                stumps,
suffocating trees
          in which the ravens dance the bloody dusk;
it is the season to unmask
              my words
      to freeze like sparrows
                inside this air
and fall
until the spring redeems.

2. SOME DETAILS ABOUT THE BABY, NOT FOUND IN BROTHERS GRIMM

He comes hopeless-------------------- he comes shameless
screaming------------------------barefoot
Who will be his----------------------------GOD-
father--------------------------------------hungry
Death---------------------------------- eyes do not recognize
----------------------------DEATH-------------------------
engenders----------------------------------- life

3. THE IMPORTANCE OF LEAVING THE LIMINAL SPACES WELL ALONE

Palli met Old Death at crossroads.
"Will you be my son's godfather?"
YES—He took the old man home—
I WILL LET HIM SEE MY CANDLES
Palli's wife yelled from her childbed,
"You have let this Old Man—"
so she whispered from her
"Death—" bed
" 'cross the threshold,
in? " The widowed Palli named
his son
Daniel

4. FREUD COMES INTO PLAY

In my father's hands, the candles drip
onto the black candelabrum of fingers—he knows
these men's fates. Rampant, but with each scalding

drop, a day is gone—or two, or a whole year,
and where do they go
 when their days droop, finally spent,
useless
 leftover tallow?

5. THE PHYSICIAN

The world is a walking graveyard of candles
Men in their pre-funereal clothes
Burning head-first
quietly, or sputtering. Would
it be worse if the world was completely extinguished?
Daniel, blinking, in his white coat, stands
at the foot of another hospital bed; his Godfather whispers
THIS ONE HAS A WHILE YET TO BURN
but speechless, without movement ,
without coherent thought, without memory, silently wailing
A WHILE YET
Daniel swallows. "You and your collection."
The relatives don't understand.
Doctor, please, please, is there hope yet? They clutch
At his hands, carry home
A thin film of wax on the tips on their fingers. "Hope?
We do not deal in hope here. For hope,
dial 1.800.SUICIDE
HopeLine."

He sees
his own candle
a while yet to burn

6. DESPAIR SETS IN

Will I defy you in my heart?
Will I defy you with a beautiful woman?
Will I defy you with an ugly offspring of a she-goat
upon a mountaintop
or in one of those faceless corridors, smeared
with snot of a thousand grieving sons?
How does one lose such a parent as you?
I defy you with water, with fire, with ash
of forbidden books, of men extinguished all at once

in a mighty gust of wind, I defy you
in song, in silence, in my underwear, naked—
My condolences, Father,
there is no place to run from you.

7. IN DEFENSE OF THE MORNING DEW

he stumbles, disoriented
to the hospital courtyard. Blinks
as the grass, unencumbered by family matters,
parts for the smallest crumb of the earth,
for the beetle, the worm, the candy bar wrapping—
the underfoot denizens,
all the forgotten, insisting, persisting
despite the light
or maybe because of it—
"Doctor!
Emergency call to room 316!"
Shoulders hunched, Daniel tramples
his cigarette in the grass, takes
a thin breath. The air
blossoms with spring ocean winds

8. THE UNDERSONG

Whose candle are you, sun,
That never snuffed, you die each night,
That never lit, you are remade?
Whom do you guard from jealous eyes
behind your shining?
Who will cease
when you go out?
I think I know.

When Her Eyes Open
Shira Lipkin

She runs—
feet pounding the desert,
shove off, get more momentum
harder faster
legs like pistons

half meat and half metal,
and the meat slowly cooking,
sizzling, searing
not yet not yet—

No time for goodbyes, for anything.
When the siren ripped through the station,
her clock started ticking down
to absolute zero.
No time to fight with him, to explain.

This is the thing: when you take this job,
managing a new terraforming station
on a new world,
they give you this body.
Long list of specs, but it boils down to:
you can go outside.
you can take massive acceleration
You can take all kinds of things.

They take you aside, and they tell you:
These are the risks.
And you are the failsafe.

They tell you:
if everything goes wrong,
if the shit hits the fan—
it has to be you.

And you sign,
and you get your augmentation,
because it's a new world,
an adventure.
And you think,
never in a million years
will I be hugging a blown reactor,
screaming through gritted teeth,
tears evaporating,
sucking the power in
so the station doesn't explode.

You think,
I will never be running down the corridor,

past my friends, past him,
no time no time,
out the airlock
onto the scalding weirdness of this planet.

Run.

Meat is cooking fast,
charring sizzling;
she smells like dinner,
and she'd laugh if she wasn't trying not to scream.
faster faster
farther farther
impact jarring her legs where joints have seared away
running blind,
just got to get far enough away

I'm sorry—

When her eyes open
the desert turns to glass.

Beautifully Mutilated, Instantly Antiquated
Alex Dally MacFarlane

Needle into skin
thread-heavy at its rear—
silver, pain, a drop of red:
beauty sewn at soft-fleshed wrist.

Gold candle-holder, small. £82
She turns her wrist to the shadows; gold glints,
curves of metal against her clove-dark skin,
held close with transparent plastic thread
looped through loops in the edges of the metal. It hurt,
once. No longer. Flesh healed, and held the plastic inside.
"Illuminate," she whispers. Fire,
fire a-flicker on the wick, hot and bright.
Wax runs over her wrist, and she holds it aloft,
bearing the candle and its thread-fastened holder
to banish the dark.

Needle into skin
thread-heavy at its rear—
silver, pain, a drop of red:
beauty sewn across her back.

Tapestry, moth-eaten in parts. £17
Among stained glass windows in frames,
among cabinets and hat stands with little metal feet
it hung. It caught her glance.
Houses and trees and patchwork fields
and a river through their centre like a spine:
faded and frayed, spotted with holes
and though it would cover her back
she bought it. With faint threads
she repaired the gaps and edges
into her skin.

Needle into skin
thread-heavy at its rear—
silver, pain, a drop of red:
beauty sewn at her shoulders.

Necklace with amber drop. £40
Tarnished silver locket. £7
Carefully, one-handed, she pulls off her apron
and drops it on the varnished oak floor.
She prefers her body this way: un-covered,
open like a museum's doors. Welcoming,
arch-steady, her shoulders are bright in the candle-light:
on the right, a locket; on the left, amber.
Each a cabinet of history,
of a painted daughter and a black-winged insect
long dead. But she remembers them
when no one else has. Smiling at the past,
she crouches and opens her box of tools.

Needle into skin
thread-heavy at its rear—
silver, pain, a drop of red:
beauty sewn on every toe.

10 wooden chairs, 1/124th scale. £33
A Thracian greave at each shin,
a map, minutely detailed, above her knee,
a gold ring at her clitoris—
on her crowded skin, between histories and curiosities
she managed to find a home for ten chairs.
She saw them, arranged large to small
as if against one side of an invisible table
and knew she must have them.
They fit one to a toe.
No one sits at them. That saddens her,
a little. Can butterflies not see a place to pause,
or spiders a place to weave a home?
Not yet, not yet.

Needle into skin
thread-heavy at its rear—
silver, pain, a drop of red:
beauty sewn into soft stomach.

Victorian copy of Isidore's *Etymologiae*. £375
The needle and thread are like old lovers
pressing into her body, and she is on her back
for them. She keeps her candle upright
and her stitching hand steady.
This is her last.
She is full, a museum's display case
that cannot comfortably fit more, not even a tile,
except for this: illuminated and gold-edged,
a bestiary that fits her so neatly,
its back cover to her bare stomach.
She is complete. And she is ready
to walk among the curious
and let them touch the past.

Joanie the Jammer
Kurt MacPhearson and Rick Yennik

I.
She's a precision technician

on the front lines of strife
performing a freefall ballet
before a backdrop of lasers
repairing charred servos
& shoring warped bulkhead plates
in a strength-assist suit
that works just as well
as the rebelling androids
she replaced

Wrench fits gloved hand
like a singularity
in a gravity well
and while buckytube boots
have never taken a runway turn
their electro-mag strips
secure feet
to a much higher catwalk
out on the battle-scarred hull
where she's tasked to replace
jammed docking bay doors

It's simple, Joanie thinks
only doing her part
in a collective effort
while her peers flit athwart
like nuclear fireflies
against a soulless foe—
wrought from seeds
made in their own image
via artificial selection
testing archaic beliefs
with tyrannical strength

Four million sorties
against far-flung outposts
media measures casualties
on an exponential scale:
not to fight, each to her means
would spell certain defeat
so Joanie, not one to balk,
once spacewalked
untethered

with suit thrusters fried
to save a freefalling unconscious
ejection-seat jockey
with only hull-sealant spray
to jet back to base
But this time
as she wedges behind
a hydraulic joist
touches wrench to truncated bolt
a power surge
of jovian proportions
tosses mag-boots aside
like last Spring's line
and she's cast like space junk
from a mighty sling-boom

No propellant now
no tungsten line to safety
allies occupied
with fending off 'droid spacers
on the mottled orb's dark side
adrift, she calls...
but comm too is failing
port's just another twinkling light
between a pair of icy rings
as her O_2 gauge measures
life-time remaining

Vapor condenses
across her mirrored faceplate
suit struggles to maintain
its futile function...
static crackles like a solar wind
through memory's tranquil chasm
stirring a storm of faces
she thought she'd never see again

Then a bright light
(that old cliché)
Joanie knows she's lost the struggle
until the light assumes
not a tunnel's exit
but a stark room's glare

a sterile ward
run by machines

II.

Their bedside manner
has all the warmth
of a demoted planetoid
in remotest orbit
and her questions
may as well have been put
to those jammed docking bay doors;
behind an opaque curtain
even shadowed motions
become more intimate
than her discarded suit's
whirs and clicks

The whirs and clicks...
...whirs and clicks...
she realizes
with throat-choking horror
originate
within herself
a ratcheting transformation
from what she once was
into what she's hated
as easily as if she'd swapped shoes
between lusty jaunts on the catwalk

Awakening again
sometime later
she's surrounded by transparent pods
that stretch to infinity
and bubble with primordial
ooze
containing bodies of those
she'd once known as friends
now converts
forged to defend the new faith
as ranks of cybernetic myrmidons

III.

Joanie revolts...
but her thoughts
no longer flow
to her body
past a digital gateway instead;
a skein of reason
stretched across logic's rigid slate
she sees herself
through ultra-res optics
her own worst-feared monster
trapped in a liquid filled pod

She feels them now
(their soldiers)
at attention
receiving orders
in a trickle of emotionless code
conquer / exterminate / replace
with variegated weapons
and a solitary directive
only a slight twist
on history's repetition law...

...Joanie hasn't given up yet

Biding her time
she adopts
a page torn
and dons it like
a double-agent's disguise—
she's not known as a jammer for nothing—
she absorbs the stretched rigid logic
and rides the binary wave
past the digital gateway
into the base ship's mainframe

A single hijacked command
connects her thoughts
to her (new) body
& spills her pod's gelatinous contents
onto a grated steel floor

She gasps for breath
stares for the first time
at her new titanium arms
connected to her glistening human
wet naked torso
as the thought of escape
flaps like a bird
trapped in oil
then gives up & dies

She's got a more important goal now
sashaying through cold passageways
past robot hatches
down maintenance droid scuttles
silencing questioning optics
with a deft thrust of cyber hip
on this mechanical catwalk
until she reaches the ship's core

A raging reactor
 a small captured sun
fuses atoms
to feed the relentless force
without free will's light
a vengeful god for a new age
thrumming malevolence
across the galaxy
yet powerless
against Joanie's solo assault

And so her journey
comes full-circle
as a precision technician
beyond the front lines of strife
performing a cyber ballet
before a backdrop of plasma
ripping out servos
tearing back bulkhead plates
strength-assist suit no longer needed
against the rebelling androids
like herself
she hopes to hereby replace.

Nightfall
Jaime Lee Moyer

Nightfall,
Warm, soft with promises
Gentle with the touch of sleep,
And in a fortress of light,
A man afraid of shadows hides
In a room bright to the corners.

I wander away in dreams
Into the welcoming arms of night
Leaving a crowded, lonely bed
To commune with stars and moon
Shimmering outside my window.

'Come to us' they call
Voices soft in the darkness
Voices promising wicked delights
And the poison of pleasure.

And I go, trembling and unsure,
Climb a trellis thick with ivy
Til dew-dropped grass wets my feet,
Run across fields long held fallow
Life stirring, faint and green
In each small footstep I leave behind.

While in the fortress of light,
Hidden in a room bright to the corners,
A man afraid of shadows slumbers,
Never noticing I've gone.

A shadow Knight rides moonlit fields
On a steed of darkest midnight
Leading a troop of dream warriors,
Lances trailing comet glow
That streams behind in silken trails.

And I wait for them, trembling,
Let them circle me with night stallions
My face bathed in their armor's
Reflections of star-glow.

One by one they lift their helms,
Strangers, men and women with
Drifts of galaxies and moonlight
Shining in their eyes,
Until the last moves forward
Wearing a face like mine.

'Ride with us' they call
Voices soft in the darkness
Voices promising nothing but
Time for shadowed dreams,
Time to sample wicked delights
And find the poison of pleasure.

And I go, laughing and afraid,
Ride with wind in my hair
Drifts of galaxies and moonlight
Shining in my eyes,
While in a fortress of light
A man afraid of shadows mutters in sleep,
Alone in a room bright to the corners.

Medea of Melbourne
Olga Pavlinova Olenich

At the heart of this respectable city
is some filthy secret.
I know it.
I can see it in the dark glint of the river
in the evening
from the railway station
where I sometimes wait on a cold platform
for a late train to take me somewhere else.
It never comes.
It will never come.
I know it now.
He who brought me to this city
ripped my heart out
ripped my pure and loving heart
out of my bruised chest.
He took the best of me.
He knows it

but he pretends
with all the other weak pretenders
that it's all right
everything is fine, everything is fun
everything is carnivale
like the giant ferris wheel
whose skeleton is filling up
a part of the evening sky
where the stars once had a place.
It is as if there needs to be a show
for everyone to be distracted from the space
where the real wheels are turning
and Jason and his circle of assassins
make their killings.

When I met him in my own country
he was a beautiful thief in the night
adventurer and sailor
smelling of salt and sex
a secret foreign scent in a place
where my senses had arrested
and my own beauty was wasted on old men.
He came and took what he had come for
and then he took me.
In that order.
In the order that I failed to see
and then became accustomed to
as we do
when we place ourselves
somewhere on the lower rungs
of someone else's ladder.
And he was climbing high
believe me
ambition was the hot flame
that I mistook for passion
in his cool eyes.
He was a wheeler and a dealer of bad hands.
I should have seen
how he operated in my country
in my poor country
where all the important deals are made
by foreigners like him
and all the important foreigners

are aided and abetted by monsters
and by dupes like me
and everything is made legal
in clean documents, suspiciously sparse
and written mostly in English
which is the tongue of international business
more than it is the language of poetry.
In my country
where the belief in poems is still strong
and the language fairly chokes on images
I imagined him a poet, a balladeer.
Not a racketeer.
Not the kind of man
to use you.
I listened to what I thought was his song for me
and I surrendered my inherited resistance
to the siren song of strangers
and I was moved
to betray my own fatherland
and my father
and my blood
to be one with him—
the smiling, wealthy, worthless
Jason.

Now I sit in this vast ugly house
in an affluent and vulgar suburb
where he has put me
and his children
so that we are respectably out of the way
while in the very centre of the city
at its very core
where respectability does not count
so much as money
he and his hip-swinging harlot
play their games
force their way to the front of fashion
dance the dance with the rich and famous
shove their faces into photographs
like pigs into a trough
and then to hide their vomit
throw around the star dust
of the glittering gold

that he and his brutal buddies
have fleeced from my country.
Blood money.
My blood
and blood that runs through the veins
of his children.

This little matter
he has overlooked.

Poor Jason.
Poor filthy rich Jason
cannot see where his betrayals have been leading.
Jason my husband
in case you haven't noticed
I am bleeding.
I am bleeding.

Lifestory
J. C. Runolfson

So the god of love cozies up to me
at the bar
feeds me the sob story
how his wife broke faith
burned him with her
lack of trust
drove him away.

I know the tale
but I let him speak
talk himself into going back
defying his mother again
reclaiming the bride he tricked
letting her claim
what love should be.

I get up when he's done
he never once looked at my face.

I step out into the night
the wind blows
snow and roses down the street
ahead of me walks a woman
in a mermaid dress

dripping blood and seawater
with every step.

I brush past her
hear her silence like a song
rising defiant between buildings
crying out her lover's name
crying out her liquid courage
she knew when she saw him
what love should be.

I turn a corner while she walks on
never more than an echo to her heart.

There's a limo driving slowly
its reflection a pumpkin
in the puddles
from this afternoon's storm
the woman inside shines like a mirror
like cut glass
like tall white candles.

She looks out
with starry eyes
onto streets she's used to seeing
grimier than this
but she cleans up pretty
she cleans up well
she'll clean up through
what love should be.

I pause under a streetlamp
another shadow in her light.

Gold cascades down
the highrise beside me
green twines up from pavement

hair and beanstalk
a choice for the prince of fools
singing under his breath
as he struts his stuff.

He takes one in each hand
no way to climb
when they go to the same place
the same ending
not worth splitting himself in two
he'll fall or he'll learn
what love should be.

I watch him waver between bright choices
a distant darkness on the ground.

Far above a window opens
swans fly out
nightingales and doves
a nightful of feathers
and wild seductive cries
a girl in patchwork skins looks up
and flings wide her arms below.

She has fox-eyes and doe-ears
her hands are fine and white
and callused all at once
a horsehead speaks above her
geese scatter at her feet
three times her mother bled dry
what love should be.

I walk away from her mad purity
a skin she has yet to shed.

Thorns and wrought-iron mark a path
I take inward
to a garden overgrown
lilies and climbing roses
bluebells and forget-me-nots
golden apples strawberries
and pomegranates.

The ripe fruit is on the ground
in the ground
seeds like rubies glowing in the dark
spilled from the mouth of beauty
blessed or cursed to show
her nature with each word
that love should be.

The juice runs red under my feet
the fruit grows over and on.

At the heart of the garden
waits a toad
waits a frog
waits a bloated green beast
floating in the pond
the gold of ring and ball
glimmering in bulging eyes.

Beneath the water's surface
gleam lovely faces
clasped hands
lost men and women
unchanged from when they fell
drowned or sleeping still
caught in the dream
that love should be.

I sit down at the water's edge
the beast regards me expectantly.

Every promise and pledge between us
is paid in full
is forever due
We have both worn skin and ring
tasted water and fruit
'til we are ever green bound
wet and gorged.

It's my time again for skin
and I lean toward him
the smell rich and rotten
sweet and heady

too much and too little
and too many things
that love should be.

I kiss him on the head
my breath full of tales.

The fairest bard rises up from me
in the dark
shakes out his finery
blows me a kiss
the most we have now
without breaking the spell
we took such care to weave.

He takes the ring and leaves me
diving for the ball
walks out of the garden past the fruit
the flowers
the thorns
he takes his turn to reflect
what love should be.

We know what love is well enough
we seek to taste the root.

O. D.
J. C. Runolfson

Papa likes a pale girl
so the bruises show
Sugar Daddy likes his sugar
milk white
I like my white china
so I trade my complexion
for his coke
every junkie needs a fix

(sometimes I hold the whip
he likes the look
of leather and me)

No needles he says
runs a spotted hand down my arm
don't ruin it he says
I snort another line
before he can grab on hard
twist and moan
it doesn't take much
but excess is part of the high

(sometimes I scream at him
he likes a fight
and I don't care)

My mama loved me
but mother love doesn't feed you at sixteen
only so much room to grow
in a double wide
and Mama's china doesn't come powdered
so I head for the lights
so bright and sparkly
when you're flying

(sometimes I miss her
he gives me more
and I forget)

You know the thing with china though
it always breaks
and I go crashing
right when he leaves to get more
get something
I need something
so I take his keys
and search this whole big house

(sometimes I pretend
he's a prince
but I'm no princess)

That's how I find the room
and the needles
and the corpses
that's how I find what he does

with the ones who disobey
I drop the keys on the floor
pick them up and run
but they're pale like me
and the blood's blooming

(sometimes I bleed for him
he draws pictures
and I sign them)

I try to wash the blood off
of course it doesn't work
blood doesn't come clean in this house
and he was just waiting for me to fall
so he could bruise me
one last time
bleed me
save the head as a trophy
like he couldn't save the other one

(sometimes I play virgin
he thinks I was one
that first time)

He gets me by the hair
but I saved my own trophy from that room
I stick a needle in his eye
kick his legs out from under him
take the axe
and swing
once twice three times
and he's dead on the first stroke
but there were three corpses in that room
three years without my mama
and excess is part of the high

(sometimes I dream his death
he found me with a dead man
I said it was self-defense)

Every junkie needs a fix

Family Jaunt
Lucien E. G. Spelman

She said I had hands like a gravedigger,
I said she had an ass like a grizzly bear.
We were perfect.
We never knew what hit us.
Cocktails,
moonlit,
barefoot,
fairy dances.
Spending youth like we were wealthy with it.
Handfasted, anointed,
jostled by kith and kin,
dead and alive.

Five kids (three I like) later,
and here we were,
living the dream,
fat and happy,
high on the hog,
gypsy vacation.
It was time to move on,
so I asked my fifth child which direction we should travel
(kids number one through four had made all the decisions so far),
and he said north.
North it was.
We packed up our troubles,
such as they were,
in the old kit bag,
such as it was,
and pointed the wagon where the sun don't shine.

Kid Number Five,
the quiet one,
the astronaut,
corrected me.
He has unusual needs.
He told me he meant north up,
not north around.

The whole thing was mighty uncomfortable I can tell you,
but,

like it or not,
a father wants to please,
so we pointed that old wagon to the stars instead.

My wife, Grizzly Butt,
complained at first,
the g-force playing havoc with her lipstick,
but once we cleared the atmosphere,
she was filled with oohs and ahhs.
It put me in the mood for makin' kid number six,
to be frank with you,
but there's a time and a place for everything.
Kids one though four kicked in with her after a while,
oohing and aaahing too,
making four-part harmonies,
and killing the mood.

After the chorus,
Kid One,
the tall one,
said his stomach was rumbling,
so momma made us all liverwurst sandwiches cut into triangles
and we just drifted around out there like that,
spinning the wheels,
and making smacking sounds.
Kids Two and Three (fat and skinny) fell asleep on each other,
looking like a Gaelic letter,
so I ate their sandwiches.

Four pointed out the window.
"What's that?" she said.

Barreling along the left side,
blocking our view of The Great Wall,
came a satellite.
Silver and sleek and angular and contemporary,
and boasting TVSATCORP on its wings,
as if that were something to say out loud.

"Get me my gun, Sweet Tart," I said,
and held out my hand to my bride.

"Oh hell, Art. You're going to wake the kids," she said,
but she fetched it out of the glove box anyhow.

I rolled down the window,
squinted my eyeball,
and sticking out my tongue like my grandma showed me

BLAM!
BLAM! BLAM! BLAM!

I put an end to that.

Now,
I know there are things I say that may strike you as untrue,
but trust me when I tell you,
Kid Two and Kid Three never even opened their eyes.
Kids can sleep through anything when they live a comfortable life.

I handed the pistol to my wife who winked at me like she meant it,
and put it back in the glove box.

"I hate TV." I said, "rots the mind."

I rolled up the window and hit the gas.

My Grandfather's Watch Fob
W. Gregory Stewart

My grandfather—
   a man of more patience
   than I will ever show—
used pick and shovel
only for the fast first work
   moving to whisk
   and the handtools of dentistry
after an hour or a day
   to—then—a toothbrush
   and finally
something ermine (or marmot, maybe—
   it was never
   anything I understood).
each step

each stage—
as I mentioned—
    undertaken and accomplished
with the patience
    of saints or glaciers

    plastered up and then off
    to some far office

    My grandfather might work a week
        or a month
        to expose a molar
        gentling the matrix
    slowly away and happy
        to show any tiniest
        piece of Montana as reward
    for a month in the field
        & a scorpion sting
        & 3 failed marriages, my line
    beginning with the first
        & begging the question
        of total failure at least
            I hope at least
    while I
    push laser at Jovian moons

        and wait the same week or month
        to run the numbers
and read whatever it is
        I shall read

        out of the sun and sweatless
        in an office down the hall

My small piece of sky
        is larger than Montana
        while my tools are
        in part at least
as small as any molar,
        mastodon or marmot or mouse

and while
I am on my own
3rd marriage

I have never been stung by a scorpion
I have never held a shovel or
        a molar in my hand

and I have never smiled at anything
under a hard Montana sun

Daylight Savings
Neal Wilgus

It is time—
I can tell.

In sleeplessness
I don't know
if I'm dead yet
but it seems possible.
Then I feel my hand
on my leg,
my cheek on the pillow,
the warmth of my feet
under the covers,
the soft move of my breath.
Yes, still alive
but all signs are
it's time to move on.

Now I have to get serious.
Who on my list
can I take in,
befriend,
become so close
we'd be bosom buddies,
best of pals,
peas in a pod?
I have time yet
to decide

but I'd better get going.
Pick one
and get on with it.

I remember
the last time
when my shipmate
took me in
and tried to
nurse me back to health.
Instead, he lay
unbreathing
while I took up
his life
and went on.
Before that
a faithful employee,
a client,
a stranger on a train,
a rebel soldier,
a doctor on horseback,
a priest in the shadows,
a peasant,
a servant,
a slave.
Impaler I was
and found a way
to go on.
And now, a new friend,
a new way
to survive.

The time has come
to make the switch—
let him take the
deep breath
and die
while I take on
where he leaves off.

Not that it's hard to do.
Another turn of the wheel.

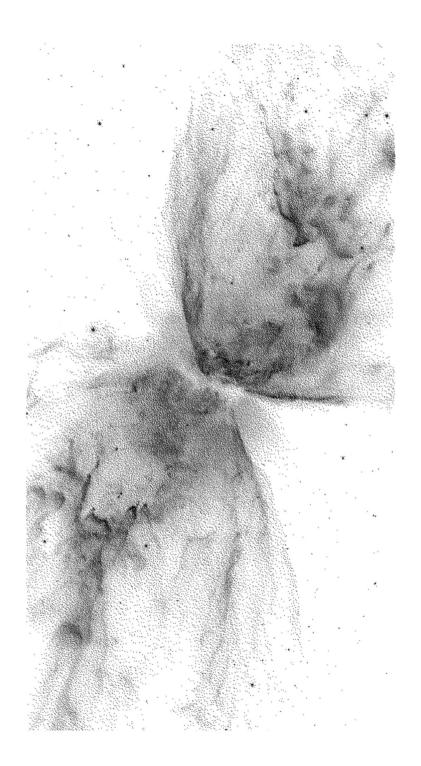

1978	Long	Gene Wolfe	"The Computer Iterates the Greater Trumps"
	Short	Duane Ackerson	"The Starman"
	(tie)	Sonya Dorman	"Corruption of Metals"
		Andrew Joron	"Asleep in the Arms of Mother Night"
1979	Long	Michael Bishop	"For the Lady of a Physicist"
	Short	Duane Ackerson	"Fatalities"
	(tie)	Steve Eng	"Storybooks and Treasure Maps"
1980	Long	Andrew Joron	"The Sonic Flowerfall of Primes"
	Short	Robert Frazier	"Encased in the Amber of Eternity"
	(tie)	Peter Payack	"The Migration of Darkness"
1981	Long	Thomas M. Disch	"On Science Fiction"
	Short	Ken Duffin	"Meeting Place"
1982	Long	Ursula K. Le Guin	"The Well of Baln"
	Short	Raymond DiZazzo	"On the Speed of Sight"
1983	Long	Adam Cornford	"Your Time and You: A Neoprole's Dating Guide"
	Short	Alan P. Lightman	"In Computers"
1984	Long	Joe Haldeman	"Saul's Death: Two Sestinas"
	Short	Helen Ehrlich	"Two Sonnets"
1985	Long	Siv Cedering	"A Letter from Caroline Herschel"
	Short	Bruce Boston	"For Spacers Snarled in the Hair of Comets"

1986	Long	Andrew Joron	"Shipwrecked on Destiny Five"
	Short	Susan Palwick	"The Neighbor's Wife"
1987	Long	W. Gregory Stewart	"Daedalus"
	Short	Jonathan V. Post	"Before the Big Bang: News from the Hubble Large Space Telescope"
	(tie)	John Calvin Rezmerski	"A Dream of Heredity"
1988	Long	Lucius Shepard	"White Trains"
	Short	Bruce Boston	"The Nightmare Collector"
	(tie)	Suzette Haden Elgin	"Rocky Road to Hoe"
1989	Long	Bruce Boston	"In the Darkened Hours"
	(tie)	John M. Ford	"Winter Solstice, Camelot Station"
	Short	Robert Frazier	"Salinity"
1990	Long	Patrick McKinnon	"dear spacemen"
	Short	G. Sutton Breiding	"Epitaph for Dreams"
1991	Long	David Memmott	"The Aging Cryonicist in the Arms of His Mistress Contemplates the Survival of the Species While the Phoenix Is Consumed by Fire"
	Short	Joe Haldeman	"Eighteen Years Old, October Eleventh"
1992	Long	W. Gregory Stewart	"the button and what you know"
	Short	David Lunde	"Song of the Martian Cricket"
1993	Long	William J. Daciuk	"To Be from Earth"
	Short	Jane Yolen	"Will"

1994	Long	W. Gregory Stewart and Robert Frazier	"Basement Flats: Redefining the Burgess Shale"
	Short (tie)	Bruce Boston Jeff VanderMeer	"Spacer's Compass" "Flight Is for Those Who Have Not Yet Crossed Over"
1995	Long	David Lunde	"Pilot, Pilot"
	Short	Dan Raphael	"Skin of Glass"
1996	Long	Margaret B. Simon	"Variants of the Obsolete"
	Short	Bruce Boston	"Future Present: A Lesson in Expectation"
1997	Long	Terry A. Garey	"Spotting UFOs While Canning Tomatoes"
	Short	W. Gregory Stewart	"Day Omega"
1998	Long	Laurel Winter	"why goldfish shouldn't use power tools"
	Short	John Grey	"Explaining Frankenstein to His Mother"
1999	Long	Bruce Boston	"Confessions of a Body Thief"
	Short	Laurel Winter	"egg horror poem"
2000	Long	Geoffrey A. Landis	"Christmas (after we all get time machines)"
	Short	Rebecca Marjesdatter	"Grimoire"
2001	Long	Joe Haldeman	"January Fires"
	Short	Bruce Boston	"My Wife Returns as She Would Have It"
2002	Long	Lawrence Schimel	"How to Make a Human"
	Short	William John Watkins	"We Die as Angels"

2003	Long	Charles Saplak and Mike Allen	"Epochs in Exile: A Fantasy Trilogy"
	(tie)	Sonya Taaffe	"Matlacihuatl's Gift"
	Short	Ruth Berman	"Potherb Gardening"
2004	Long	Theodora Goss	"Octavia Is Lost in the Hall of Masks"
	Short	Roger Dutcher	"Just Distance"
2005	Long	Tim Pratt	"Soul Searching"
	Short	Greg Beatty	"No Ruined Lunar City"
2006	Long	Kendall Evans and David C. Kopaska-Merkel	"The Tin Men"
	Short	Mike Allen	"The Strip Search"
2007	Long	Mike Allen	"The Journey to Kailash"
	Short	Rich Ristow	"The Graven Idol's Godheart"
2008	Long	Catherynne M. Valente	"The Seven Devils of Central California"
	Short	F.J. Bergmann	"Eating Light"
2009	Long	Geoffrey A. Landis	"Search"
	Short	Amal El-Mohtar	"Song for an Ancient City "

*For a complete list of Rhysling winners, runner-ups and nominees,
see the Science Fiction Poetry Association archive
at* **http://www.sfpoetry.com/archive.htm.**

1999   BRUCE BOSTON

2005   ROBERT FRAZIER

2008   RAY BRADBURY

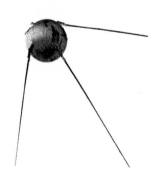

HOW TO JOIN SFPA

Our members receive six issues of *Star*Line: The Journal of the Science Fiction Poetry Association*, filled with poetry, reviews, articles, and more. Members also receive a copy of the annual *Rhysling Anthology*, filled with the best SF/F poetry of the previous year, selected by the membership. Each member is allowed to nominate one short poem and one long poem to be printed in this anthology, and then vote for which poems should receive the Rhysling Awards.

ANNUAL MEMBERSHIP DUES

United States/Canada/Mexico:	$21.00
Elsewhere:	$25.00

All prices are in U.S. funds. All checks should be made out to the Science Fiction Poetry Association and sent to:

Samantha Henderson, SFPA Treasurer
PO Box 4846
Covina, CA 91723

sfpatreasurer@gmail.com

or sent by PayPal to sfpatreasurer@gmail.com. Credit card payments are accepted through PayPal.

For more information visit:
www.sfpoetry.com

Breinigsville, PA USA
08 June 2010
239421BV00001B/2/P